# CROSSBEARER

ALSO BY JOE ESZTERHAS

*The Devil's Guide to Hollywood*

*Hollywood Animal*

*American Rhapsody*

*Charlie Simpson's Apocalypse*

*Nark*

# CROSSBEARER

A

MEMOIR

OF

FAITH

JOE ESZTERHAS

St. Martin's Press
New York

www.stmartins.com

*Book design by Abby Kasan*

*Epigraphs on pages 1 and 77 are taken from the Holman Christian Standard Bible.*

Library of Congress Cataloging-in-Publication Data

Eszterhas, Joe.
    Crossbearer : a memoir of faith / Joe Eszterhas.—1st ed.
      p. cm.
    ISBN-13: 978-0-312-38596-5
    ISBN-10: 0-312-38596-X
  1. Eszterhas, Joe—Religion.   2. Eszterhas, Joe—Health.   3. Screenwriters—United
States—Biography.   4. Throat—Cancer—Patients—United States—Biography.   I. Title.
    PS3555.S98Z46  2008
    812'.54—dc22
    [B]
                                                                    2008024268

First Edition: October 2008

10   9   8   7   6   5   4   3   2   1

FOR MY MOTHER—MARIA ESZTERHAS . . .

AND FOR NAOMI, SUNLIGHT

# FAITH

✝

*Therefore, since we have been declared righteous by faith, we have
peace with God through our Lord Jesus Christ. Also through Him,
we have obtained access by faith into this grace in which we stand,
and we rejoice in the hope of the glory of God.*

**—PAUL'S LETTER TO THE ROMANS 5:1-2**

THIS IS HOW I FOUND GOD . . . or how God found me.

In March of 2001, Naomi and I moved our boys back to Ohio, where she and I had grown up. We wanted the boys to live in a more traditional environment. Hypodermic needles were being found in the Malibu park where our boys were playing; police said there was a heroin problem among thirteen-year-olds; ten-year-old little girls were chatting about gang bangs.

In April of 2001, only weeks after we got back to Ohio, I was diagnosed with throat cancer. I was twelve years old when I'd started smoking, fourteen when I'd started drinking. I was now fifty-six.

They cut out 80 percent of my larynx at the Cleveland Clinic. They put a tube down my throat so I could breathe. I couldn't speak. I used a child's blackboard to communicate. They told me I had to stop smoking and drinking immediately—*immediately!*—or I'd die.

But . . . after forty-four years of smoking, to stop right now—*immediately?* Not a single day had gone by in those forty-two and forty-four years when I didn't smoke or have something alcoholic to drink. And I was now drinking a fifth of Tanqueray or Jack Daniel's or Cuervo every day—plus beer, wine, champagne.

And now I had to stop.

Just stop.

Just like that.

Right now.

Immediately!

*I knew I couldn't do it.*

But I loved my wife and children. I adored my wife and children. So I tried. I stopped smoking. I stopped drinking. I was trying my best to stay alive. I was trying my best not to die.

*And I knew I couldn't do it.*

It was a blazing hot late spring day in Ohio. Ninety-two in the shade. I hadn't had a cigarette or a drink in a month.

I was going crazy. I was jittery. I twitched. I trembled. I had no patience for anything. I yelled at Naomi and the boys. My heart was skipping beats. I had no appetite. I had trouble swallowing anything. The trache was still down my throat. I was nauseated, my knees were weak.

Every single nerve ending was demanding a drink and a cigarette.

All I thought about every hour of every day was having a drink and a cigarette.

I left the house and started to walk. I walked as fast as I could. I was too old to run. I was trying to outwalk my cravings and my addictions. I was trying to outwalk panic. I was trying to outwalk my own self-destructiveness.

I was trying to outwalk death.

I wanted so very badly, so painfully badly, to run back to my house and get in the car and drive down a couple of blocks to the Coyote Café. To do a shot of tequila. Two shots of tequila. Three shots of tequila. Two iced Coronas. Three iced Coronas. Four iced Coronas. And a pack of Salem Lights.

I was sweating like a pig as I walked the little cul-de-sac streets around my house. I couldn't breathe. I was shaking so badly, I watched my hands dance. The damn bugs and mosquitoes were trying to dive and crawl into my trache, into the hole in my neck.

I started to cry. I knew I was hyperventilating. I sat down on the curb. Tears were streaming down my face now. I watched them splatter on the ground. My heart hammered so loudly, it blocked everything out except my sobs. I didn't sound human to myself. I listened to myself moaning. I sounded like a wounded animal.

I heard myself mumble something. I heard myself saying it. I couldn't believe I'd said it. I didn't know why I'd said it. I'd never said it before. Then I listened to myself say it again. And again and again.

*"Please, God, help me."*

I knew that in reality, in actual fact, I couldn't have said it or anything at all. My larynx was almost gone. That hellish tube was in there. I couldn't even whisper, let alone *say* anything. But I distinctly *heard* myself saying it again and again and again.

*"Please, God, help me."*

I was praying. Asking. Begging. For help. Begging God to help me. And I thought to myself: *Me? Asking God? Begging God? Praying?"* I hadn't even thought about God since I was a boy, yet I was listening to myself begging Him for help over and over again as I moaned in pain.

And suddenly my heart stilled. My nerve endings stopped torturing me. I stopped trembling and twitching. My hands stopped dancing. I realized that I wasn't jittery. Even the damn mosquitoes and bugs went away. My knees felt strong.

I got up off the curb and stood up. I opened my eyes. I saw a shimmering, dazzling, nearly blinding brightness that made me cover my eyes with my hands. I wiped my eyes and opened them. The brightness faded back to day. I walked back home.

*I thought I could do it now.*

It would be the greatest struggle of my life. It would be excruciatingly difficult, but with God's help, I thought I could do it.

I could defeat myself and win.

If I fought very hard.

And if I prayed.

Something happened to me on that hellish muggy day as I sat on the curb seven years ago. For a long time I didn't know how to describe what it was, but now I do.

*I was saved.*

"EVERY CANCER IS A JOURNEY," said my friend Doug, a voice specialist at the Cleveland Clinic who'd seen thousands of cancer patients. It was two weeks after my surgery. "You never know where the journey will take you, where you'll go. You'll have moments of fear, hope, pain, and, if you're lucky, joy. What's important is to go with it—*wherever* it goes. I could never say 'enjoy the ride' in this context, but that's sort of what you have to do. Yes, you can affect the safety of your journey by what you do—don't smoke, don't drink, exercise, eat fish, stay away from red meat. But a great many things on this journey will be outside your control. You have to accept that you're not entirely the driver. I wish you a successful trip."

USING THAT WORD—*saved*—didn't come naturally to me.

*Saved? Who, me? From what?*

When I was a very young reporter for *The Plain Dealer* in the late 1960s, I covered a crusade by the reverend A. A. Allen, world-renowned preacher/healer, at the Cleveland Arena. Thousands of wild-eyed faithful showed up, and I watched cynically as many of them answered the call at the altar. They tossed their crutches aside and hallelujaed tear-soaked words like "I've been saved, Jesus! Thank you, Jesus! I've been saved!"

The trouble was that the second night of the crusade, some

of the *same people* went up to the altar again, threw their crutches away again, and yelled "I've been saved, Jesus! Thank you, Jesus! I've been saved!"

Almost forty years later, I was still extremely wary of that word—*saved!*—when a young man used it at a book signing to describe what had happened to me as I sat on that curb crying and asking for God's help after my throat surgery. "You were saved that day," the young man said, and at first I thought—Oh no, please, not that holy-roller whoop-de-do again—but then, the more I thought about it, I astounded myself by thinking, Yes, that's right. I was saved.

*From what?*

From the darkness that I had been drawn to most of my life, the evil I had spent so much time and effort studying and analyzing from the time I was a young man. I had sought out and interviewed serial killers and mass murderers, trying to understand why they had done their heinous crimes. Then, later, in fiction, on the movie screen, I had plotted out the things I had learned from my interviews in films like *Jagged Edge* and *Basic Instinct.*

In some ways, I was writing about myself, I knew. Nick Curran, Michael Douglas's character in *Basic,* had gotten too close to evil, to "the flame" as Sharon Stone's character told him, "and Nicky liked it."

Like Nick Curran, I too got too close to the flame and I too liked it.

A child of the darkness, I wallowed in it . . . *all of it . . .* booze and cigarettes and coke and weed and the place where all of that led: the sexy, neon women who liked dancing on the edge just as much as I did. *I couldn't get enough of it!* At four in the morning once, in Vegas, walking up the dark stairway to yet another dark room to yet another lap dance in yet another dark club, a Hollywood producer friend walking up the stairs behind me said, "Man, you are relentless!"

Yes I was. I could never get enough of whatever it was . . . but all of it, all of what I wanted . . . was poisonous . . . both to my body and my spirit. It burned me out. I woke up not knowing where I was or who was asleep next to me.

My daughter from my first marriage, Suzi, knew what was going on, even if my first wife, Gerri, pretended that she didn't. It was Halloween night and I was in Vegas, yet again, "researching" a film, and I called Suzi to wish her happy Halloween, and Suzi said, "What are you going to do tonight, Dad?" "I don't know yet," I lied to my teenage daughter. And she laughed and said, "Right. Rage on, Dad! *Rage on!*"

And then, sitting on my curb and crying, I was saved. Truth to tell, Naomi and our four little boys saved me first . . . from *some* of it. I stopped the coke and the weed. I stopped the leggy, sexy neon women who always seemed to be around, wondering if the guy who wrote *Basic* knew what he was writing about.

But I couldn't stop the drinking and the smoking. And Naomi and our little boys couldn't help me stop, either. The enemy was inside me, literally killing me, and I couldn't do anything about it. I kept poisoning myself. I was so screwed up I thought I needed cigarettes to breathe better (really!). And alcohol was the high-octane fuel that powered me.

And then . . . for the first time since I was a boy . . . I opened my heart to God on that curb . . . and instead of turning His back on me, instead of saying, "Come on! Give me a break! Not *you*!" God entered my heart. And God saved me—from darkness. From death itself.

God saved me . . . from me.

I was in complete shock in the days and weeks after it happened, when I realized that with God's help, I could do anything, even quit smoking and drinking, even kill the ravenous twin devils who were eating me up inside, turning my body parts (I had seen the X-rays of my cancerous throat) coal-black.

I was in shock partly because I had never believed that this could happen. The fact that it *was* happening—that God was in *my* heart and I felt better than ever before—made no sense to me. I had mocked conversion, which biblical scholars define as "a change to a completely different life." I had made fun of conversion my whole life.

I had especially scoffed at deathbed conversions. I had lampooned those who claimed to have experienced deathbed conversion as gutless wimps, unable to *walk* their atheism or agnosticism. They betrayed their own beliefs, I mocked, by covering their bets in the months, weeks, or days before the final blackout.

And now here I was. Was I wimping out, too? I wondered sometimes, so afraid of dying, so "yella" as all the old he-man John Wayne movies said, that I had conjured a "yella" cross to hold on to?

I knew, though, as I thought about it, knew deep in my heart, that this was no "yella" cross. This was a cross with the image of a suffering Christ crucified. By focusing on His pain and suffering, my own pain became easier to bear. By focusing on His great courage and strength, I felt stronger and more courageous carrying my own crosses.

The idea had not yet occurred to me that I would become Jesus's crossbearer. That, in humble gratitude for helping me with my own crosses, I would try to help Him carry His.


MY SON NICK had always had a deep faith.

One night when he was very little and we were still living in

Malibu, Naomi tucked him into bed later than usual. It was a dark and windy night. The Pacific Ocean outside our windows was howling. Naomi was afraid that Nick wouldn't be able to get to sleep.

"Don't be scared," she reassured him, "I know it's dark and windy outside, but we're just across the hall from you."

The lights went out just then, and in the darkness Naomi could see the little boy's eyes. He wasn't afraid. He was smiling, his eyes shiny.

"You know what?" Nick whispered, as though he were telling her a secret. "Sometimes if it's dark and you think you're alone, you're not. Like if you get stuck in a cave by yourself and a rock suddenly falls in front of the way out and it's all dark and you can't get out, you're not alone. You know why? Because God is with you. God is always with you. You're not ever alone."

Nick was only four years old then, but he was so much smarter than I was.

I COULDN'T WRITE. I had loved writing and couldn't understand those writers who bellyached about how they had to force themselves to sit in front of their laptops.

I realized now that I had never written anything completely sober or undrugged. I'd always chain-smoked as I wrote, and in later years, I'd usually sipped white wine or coffee laced with cognac.

Now, without cigarettes or alcohol, I couldn't focus. I sat there in front of my battered old Olivetti manual typewriter and all I could think about was having a cigarette or a drink.

I typed out these words: "I have become Jack Nicholson in *The Shining,* sitting here and pretending to write."

I asked my new friend, God, to help me to write.

He didn't.

I felt hopeless.

I was disciplined, though. I went up to my office and sat in front of my typewriter every day, without fail. I was unable to write anything, but at least I had checked in for work. I was up in my office, sitting there, staring at the empty page, ready.

I had the feeling sometimes that Joe Eszterhas had died, that I had been born again as another person.

I was lucid and sober all the time. I wasn't being driven around in limos, I was driving myself around, often in a pickup truck. I didn't look like a rock-and-roller anymore, with hair down to the middle of my back, dripping with silver jewelry.

My hair was short and I wore my simple wedding band and a small silver cross around my neck. A friend of mine said I looked now "like a Ukrainian bishop."

I wasn't spending hours on the phone each day in conference calls; my voice was so ragged even the operators couldn't understand me. I wasn't having three-hour dinners with many bottles of wine; dinners took a half hour now, and I sipped Naomi's lemonade throughout.

I didn't go to rock concerts. I went to church. And I didn't go anywhere without Naomi and the boys. I couldn't even listen to rock and roll. The songs that I loved somehow brought back my cigarette and alcohol cravings.

I had always been a night person—whether it was partying, boozing, philandering, or writing, I had always preferred to do it in darkness.

Sober now, in love with my wife, trying to be the best father I could be to my little boys, walking five miles each day, I had become a day person.

A lifelong child of the night, I was a child of the light now.

I got up with the sun and, frazzled and exhausted, I went to sleep only a few hours after the sun set.

I was having a brutal time adjusting. No night had ever been long enough for me. Some days, I discovered now, were too long, boring, an endless effort to get through without booze and cigarettes.

But I would be a child of the light. Or die trying.


I DIDN'T EVEN really know how to pray. I remembered my mother saying her rosary in a whispered mumble, a parade of Our Fathers, Hail Marys, and Glory Bes speeding along under her breath.

I tried that, but after a while I found myself in a trancelike, mantric state, a condition I thought too impersonal and robotic for a talk with God. I tried speaking directly to Him, as a good old pal, but I felt too self-conscious and clumsy when I addressed Him.

Part of it was that I felt myself to be *presuming* God's favor in our new relationship. I thought to myself: Yeah, right, I reject Him so long ago, and then, after forty years of not just ignoring Him but of trashing Him in my writings, I'm suddenly back and talking to Him as though nothing had interrupted our relationship, saying, "How ya doin', God? Haven't seen you in a while, what up? Everything cool?"

I had a tweaking fear that I was trying to suck up to and shuck and jive Him, to get Him to help me—that I really didn't deserve His help or His presence in my life. Because I had not only violated his Commandments, but had even thrown my writerly sticks and stones at Him.

I had also raised two children, Steve and Suzi, now grown,

and had taught them that, at best, God was irrelevant in their lives. Suzi described herself on a college entrance questionnaire as a "pagan." When she was in high school, she walked around with a T-shirt of the crucified Christ with the word JOKER in big letters above His crown of thorns. When her high school principal, a Christian, objected to the T-shirt as inappropriate, I told him that I would sue both the school *and* him if he took any disciplinary action against Suzi and her JOKER T-shirt. Steve was seemingly oblivious to anything that had to do with God or religion (I had taught him well, obviously).

And now here I was trying to speak to the God whom I had marginalized and mocked and lampooned. How do you approach someone to whom you've done that? I didn't know what to say, so one of the first things I said was, "I'm sorry. I've acted like a colossal A-hole. I'm really, really sorry. I don't deserve to be forgiven, but please try to forgive me."

I know what you're thinking. You're thinking, He talks to God *that way*? But you see, I can't talk to Him any other way. I've never been comfortable with Thees and Thous. I'm down-to-earth, and if I'm going to talk to God as a friend, a pal, and talk to Him face-to-Face, guy to Guy, then my instinct is to talk to Him the way I talk to all my friends. That means it's very hard for me to say stuff like "Dear Lord, I beseech you to come to my aid in my hours of desperate need." I can say, instead, "Man, I'm totally up Shit Creek without a paddle for the first time in my life. I know I don't deserve it. I know I've been an eff-up, but can you help me? Can you please just sort of reach down from the Pearly Gates and give me a hand?"

Eventually, praying became easier for me. I felt more at ease speaking to God. While I didn't hear Him say anything in response to me, didn't hear anything coming from a mountaintop or a burning bush, I thought I saw Him shaking His head sometimes, or scowling at me, or looking away in disapproval.

But sometimes I thought I saw Him smiling, too, grinning a godly grin.

I could *almost* hear God saying, "Little man, you really have been *such* an A-word!"

(I think that is a good sign, a sign of respect, a sign of the new me: At least I don't quote God saying the A-word itself, just its abbreviated euphemism.)

And the "little man" I took as a sign of God's affection for me, His love of me. He was the Big Man and I was the little man, and it was just like the ball caps that my youngest son, Lukey, and I wore on Father's Day that said BIG DUDE and LITTLE DUDE.

I had learned that we were all God's children, and I viewed myself now as a returned prodigal son. I hoped to convince Him that His prodigal son loved Him.

I WANTED to go to church. I hadn't really been to church since I was a boy, but I felt a deep need now to go to church to worship God. I wanted to thank Him for the strength He was giving me to resist my cravings.

Ever since that day when I sat down in the street and cried, I felt what I could best describe as a glow in my heart. I felt that God was giving me a chance at a new and better life.

I still couldn't believe that I felt this way. I, who had scoffed at all things religious most of my life. I was the king daddy of sex and violence. I had been called a sleazemeister and a pornographer. I had even made fun of the Mormon religion on national television, telling Brian Williams that "Mormon is just a letter away from 'moron.'"

And now here I was at Holy Angels Roman Catholic Church in Bainbridge Township, Ohio, feeling God's glow in my heart, thanking Him for blessing me in my hours of need. I remembered reading long ago about Saul seeing the light on the way to Damascus and felt as if I had seen the same light in my neighborhood cul-de-sac as I sat there crying in the street that day.

Holy Angels Church was a middle- to upper-middle-class parish in an eastern suburb of Cleveland, thirty miles from downtown. Its parishioners had names like Suszkowski, Stempak, Radkowsky, Rapposelli, Rusko, Scarazzo, Holupka, Horvath, Hryb, Hajdu, ethnic names like mine. The parish was vibrant, booming, and filled with children's voices.

I felt the parishioners eyeing us as Naomi and I and the four boys sat in our pew the first few Sundays we were there. They were friendly enough, but I read their eyes. They knew who I was. They had read the newspaper or watched the television news announcing my return to Cleveland, the city where I had grown up. And now here I was, in the flesh, wearing a Cleveland Indians T-shirt and jeans, on my knees and unable to speak because the trache was still in my throat.

I watched myself through their eyes as they watched me praying and felt their thoughts: "Can you believe this? Mr. *Basic Instinct* and *Showgirls*? Hollywood Joe, here all pious at the ten o'clock Mass. Oh boy! I thought I'd seen everything! God sure does work in mysterious ways!"

THE PARISHIONERS studied me for a while, and then their natural midwestern goodness, their folksy neighborliness, opened up to me.

They stopped us after Mass on the way to doughnuts and coffee in the church basement and said things like:

"Your boys are very well behaved. You don't see that too often nowadays. You're doing something right."

And: "I'm praying for your recovery."

And: "Welcome home, Joe."

And: "You know, you never should have gone out to that darn Hollywood in the first place."

And: "My dad went to high school with you. He said you guys raised a lot of hell back then."

And: "Tell me something. You know the end of that movie *Basic Instinct,* does she kill him or not?"

And: "Do you have any old movie posters that you could sign and put up for the church auction?"

We went to a Friday night Lenten fish fry, and a man in his forties with three kids took me aside, put his arm around me, and said, "What are you writing these days?"

I explained that I was having trouble writing anything thanks to my nicotine and alcohol cravings.

He nodded, looked away, and then looked back at me and said, suddenly very animated: "You gotta keep writing. Your movies—I mean—we love *that stuff* you write. Like *that stuff* in *Basic Instinct.*"

He had the kind of smile on his face now, I noted, that we Ohioans call a "shit-eating grin."

He glanced for a second back at his kids to make sure they weren't overhearing us, and he said, "You know what I mean, right?"

I flashed my own shit-eating grin back at him and nodded.

"That-a-boy," he said, and slapped me on the back.

One Sunday morning, four ladies stopped us in the church vestibule.

They were members of Holy Angels Church's Sew Faithful Committee, and hearing of my illness, they had made something for us, they said.

They handed it to us. It was a sumptuous, beautifully sewn wall-size quilt which they had made with their own hands. It showed two huddled figures holding on to each other surrounded by a thick, dark, junglelike forest.

Naomi and I more than identified with those two figures. We recognized ourselves.

We thanked and hugged the ladies and had the quilt framed and put it up on our bedroom wall. It will be there as long as we live.

THE PASTOR of Holy Angels Church was a man in his midsixties, Father Joe. He was avuncular and friendly, and he welcomed us to his parish and told me he'd pray for my recovery. I thanked him and he hugged me.

It was time shortly afterward to baptize Luke, our baby, and Father Joe did the baptism himself, holding Lukey and blessing him, it seemed to us, with special affection.

Shortly after the baptism, *The Plain Dealer,* the local newspaper, revealed that this friendly, affectionate, devout man, Father Joe, was one of fourteen priests in the diocese being suspended for what *The Plain Dealer* said were allegations of "child sex abuse."

*Great!* Just great! I thought to myself. I come to the Midwest to give my boys a life of all-American traditional values, and the priest in our own little Mayberry, Bainbridge Township, immediately turns out to be accused of "child sex abuse."

I find God . . . and the priest who baptizes my baby boy and tells him to "renounce Satan and all his works" . . . appears in scandalous headlines. Mr. Hollywood has come home to Bainbridge Township, and his parish priest is alleged to have habits and predilections even people in Hollywood condemn.

I thought briefly about demanding a new baptism for Luke but ultimately decided that the person doing the baptizing didn't matter; the priest was only a tour guide to the mystery of faith. Luke had been blessed by God the day of his baptism, not by the all-too-human Father Joe.

Father Joe left Holy Angels not much later and was living in Florida somewhere, a gardener for a landscape company, his former parishioners whispered.

Yet this, too, had to be said about Father Joe: Holy Angels Church was beautiful. There was a grand simplicity about it. The walls were windows surrounded by trees. It was a tranquil and harmonious space where it was easy to worship God.

And it wouldn't have existed today without the efforts of Father Joe. He designed it and raised the money for it. He did all the necessary politicking with the diocese and the county commissioners.

Father Joe pretty much single-handedly built a magnificent house of God.

I asked God to bless the alleged "child sex abuser" for having accomplished that.

FATHER BOB had been Father Joe's assistant, and after Father Joe's departure, he unofficially took over Holy Angels Church.

He was in his forties, a tall, dynamic, good-looking man whose love of God and Jesus was palpable. His charisma fired up the congregation. People were *pumped* when Father Bob said the Mass. He was a lifelong Clevelander who'd grown up in a western suburb in a large family, the son of old-style ethnic parents who were often in church when he said Mass.

I could tell Father Bob knew very well who I was after I started showing up in church. I saw him watching me sometimes. He wasn't warm to me. He watched me, it seemed to me sometimes, warily, almost suspiciously, as if to say, *What are you doing here?* Or, *Are you sure you should be here?*

I was going to church each Sunday, but I wasn't going to Holy Communion. My relationship with God was too new—I didn't feel worthy to receive the body of Christ. So as Naomi got up to go to Holy Communion each Sunday, I sat there with the boys. I saw people staring at me sometimes as I sat there. I saw Father Bob watching me.

I was wrestling with my life. Would I be able to continue to resist my addictions? Would my cancer return? Would I live or die? Would I ever write anything again?

As he walked down the aisle after Mass one day, Father Bob stopped where I was standing in my pew and, out of the blue, said this to me: "Do you know what this means? This means that the best is yet to come. The best part of your life is still ahead of you!" He said nothing else, his eyes blazing away at me, and then he walked on.

I stood there for a few moments, dumbfounded, and couldn't stop thinking about what he'd said. I kept thinking about it all day. It was as though Father Bob had read my mind.

How did he know that by saying that to me, he'd answered the question that was keeping me up at night?

Who was this priest who could read my mind and whose eyes seemed to zero in on my heart and soul when he looked at me?

I knew he was a very well-respected man in the diocese (he'd be named "Catholic of the Year" a few years later). Holy Angels was almost a secondary assignment for him; his full-time job was being the vocational director for the diocese. He was the man assigned by the bishop to talk young men into joining the seminary—at a time when no one wanted to be a priest, when priests were the objects of sick jokes all over the world. And even in these difficult times, it was a job Father Bob did well. Cleveland, unlike other dioceses, had a successful seminary enrollment—no doubt greatly thanks to Father Bob's charisma and powers of persuasion.

One day, again out of the blue, he called me at home and said, "Joe, God told me to tell you this: Stop beating yourself up over the past and the things you may have done that you regret. God has given you a new life—live it."

The Sunday after that phone call, I stood up for Holy Communion. When I got up there, Father Bob peered into my heart and soul and said, "Body of Christ, Joe."

I blinked away a tear and said, "Amen." I took the host in my hand and put it in my mouth and swallowed it with my ravaged throat. I felt God's love surrounding me. God was in my heart. The body of Christ was in mine.

I looked up from my pew after bowing my head in prayer and saw Father Bob looking at me. His eyes were hawklike and fixed, and he was smiling.

His smile said, "Welcome, you made it."

Father Bob and I became friends. The depth of his love of God inspired me. He told me that a line in one of my films, *Flashdance,* had inspired him: When you give up on your dreams, you die.

So I had inspired Father Bob a long time ago to follow his dream—which was to become a priest.

And now, as a priest, he had inspired me in turn to love God and to believe that the best was yet to come in my life.

I thanked God that I had written *Flashdance*, a film that some critics had called "a T and A extravaganza."

I ASKED GOD now to grant me the greatest blessing of all.

Please, I said, let me live. Let me beat this cancer. I don't want to live for me. I'm no longer interested in all the superficial things that have always fueled my ambitions.

I want to live for Naomi and our four little boys. And for my grown kids, Steve and Suzi. I want to be here to help Naomi raise the boys. I want to be here to hold Naomi's hand as we sip lemonade on the porch and watch our boys toss the ball around in the front yard. I want to be here to hear the sweet sound of a screen door slamming.

And if you let me live, I said to God, I will do what I can for You.

I will tell the world with my ragged voice about how smoking kills and destroys lives.

I will tell the world how I killed people and destroyed lives by writing films that glorified smoking.

I will tell Hollywood that it's not enough for us to make uplifting movies about just and righteous political causes, we also have to stop making movies that literally kill people.

And I will tell the world about You—about how You changed my life and saved me—even if telling the world destroys my Hollywood career.

And I will try to write things that my four little boys can see or read and that You'll like.

And I will do my best to lead a good Christian life. I will

remember that You said, "What you do unto the least of my brethren, you do unto Me."


I HAD been a control freak all of my life in ways big and small. I had been in charge of myself and had always rebelled against anyone telling me what to do.

In grade school, the nun who was my eighth-grade teacher told me, "You're going to wind up in jail!" because I wouldn't obey her. In college, at the school newspaper, I was fired because I couldn't stand anyone editing my work. In Hollywood, I was famous as the Man Who Wouldn't Rewrite His Scripts (unless I wanted to). I tangled with directors, producers, and movie stars who wanted "input" into my writing.

I controlled all aspects of my life. My lawyers, accountants, and agents advised me, but I often overruled them. If my agents dared to make creative suggestions, I told them quickly they were there to negotiate *deals,* not third acts or endings.

I trusted very few people and rarely delegated authority. I wanted to make sure that everything was done perfectly. That meant I had to do it myself. It was a pattern that had begun when I was a child. My parents were immigrants who didn't know this strange country called America and could hardly speak English. They trusted *me* to explain America and how to deal with it. They needed *me* to get along in this new world.

That was a lot of power for a little boy.

Yet now, for the first time in my life, I gave up *all control.* I put my life in God's hands. God was in control—my life was up to His will, not mine.

I was amazed how happy I was with this new arrangement. I

didn't resent that I was no longer in charge. I felt like a thousand-pound weight had been lifted off my back.

For the first time in my life, I felt free—even though I was in a battle with cancer and my addictions.

I thanked God for freeing me, for loving me so much that He was willing to take over my life. I trusted Him—whatever He decided to do with me. I was at peace.

"St. Paul makes many references to the meaning and power of the cross in letters to the early Christian communities.

"To the Galatians, he wrote: 'May I never boast, except in the cross of our Lord Jesus Christ.'

"To the Corinthians, he called the cross a stumbling block and foolishness for unbelievers, but for those with faith, a source of new life through Jesus Christ.

"Early in the Church, the cross became the symbol of our salvation. This is why the sign of the cross is an important ritual gesture. It is quite fitting that when we gather at the church, the Body of Christ, we begin by marking ourselves with this sign, first with water of the baptismal font, then at the beginning of the liturgy, and again as we are sent forth to live the life of Christ."

Simon of Cyrene helped Jesus carry the cross on the way to his crucifixion and became, if you wanted to interpret it that way, the first crossbearer. But according to most accounts, he was "compelled" by the Romans to carry the cross. While some accounts said he had sympathy for Jesus and volunteered to help him, there was no evidence for this. Nor was there any evidence for the theory that it was Simon of Cyrene who died on the cross instead of Jesus and that it was really Simon who suffered what Jesus had suffered. If that was true (and I was sure it wasn't), it meant that Simon of Cyrene was one crossbearer who got much more than he bargained for.

Nobody compelled me to carry the cross at Holy Angels Church. I did it as a way of thanking Jesus for helping me. I felt honored to do it; it was my pleasure.

The drill for carrying the cross into and out of church before and after Mass was simple. You took it from its stand in the vestibule and carried it, leading the altar boys and the priest, to the altar, where you put it on another stand.

One Sunday morning I carried it in and tried to put it on its stand, but the cross wouldn't fit. I moved the cross around and jammed it on the stand and tilted it and swiveled it, but it didn't work. I stood at the altar trying to ram it into its stand—no go. Jesus was up there on high—swaying, wobbling, almost ready to fall, thanks to me. I saw that the parishioners were giving me the evil eye. *Just lookit that Hollywood jackass!*

I said, "Please, God, what have I done lately that You should do this to me in front of hundreds of people, looking like the klutz of the universe, a dimwit, blushing, gray-haired fuddy-duddy who has difficulty putting anything into its proper receptacle anymore?"

Father Bob finally came over to me, whispering, "Can I help you?" and with one little touch clanked the bottom of the cross into the stand.

I said, "Thank you, Father Bob," and walked back to my pew, where my wife and sons were laughing at me.

After Communion, with the body of Christ still in my mouth, I bowed my head and prayed to God like I always did— for my wife, my children, my dear departed parents, my ex-wife, our friends, etc., etc., etc.

Then I said to Him, "I don't know what I've done to make You do that to me up there. Do You have any idea how difficult it is not to have a cold beer at the ballpark when it's ninety-four degrees outside? Do You know how badly I want a cigarette after playing Ping-Pong with the boys? And three rows ahead of me right now there's a seventeen-year-old nubile sex bomb with a halter top and I haven't even noticed her. I'm doing my best to behave, okay? I'm being a good boy, I really am. I've been a bad boy all my life, granted, but I'm busting my hump here, Big Man, I really am."

When Mass was over I went and got the cross and yanked it so hard off its stand that I almost knocked the candles down. I saw Naomi and the boys yukking it up again as I passed them in the aisle.

THE BISHOP, in his infinite wisdom, moved Father Bob to another parish near the West Side suburb where he grew up.

This after Father Bob had stabilized Holy Angels and had quelled the turmoil caused by the allegations surrounding Father Joe. The affection that the parishioners felt for Father Bob had ultimately overcome their anger at the church. Father Bob had successfully tamed the rebellion rumbling in the pews of the Holy Angels worship space.

And now, just like that ("at Nero's whim," one parishioner said), Father Bob was gone. And now the parishioners were *really* angry at the church, and talk of revolution was in the incensed air at Holy Angels once again. People were whispering in the vestibule about writing letters to the bishop and signing petitions and sending e-mails and texts. More significant, some parishioners were threatening to withhold money from the

collection basket or—God forbid!—boycott the doughnut breakfast in the church basement.

Once again, though—mirabile dictu—revolution in the pews
was averted, this time by the arrival of our new (and permanent)
pastor.

Father Dan was Father Bob's age, in his early forties, and had
gone to the seminary with him, but the similarities pretty much
ended there. Father Dan wasn't strikingly good-looking: He was
almost bald and had a roundish face. He was short and sometimes
wore a goatee that made him look like a Russian revolutionary,
an unstarved Lenin in Zurich. Father Dan wasn't overtly charismatic. He spoke softly and his eyes didn't bore, hawklike, into
your soul. His eyes were shy and he more often than not glanced
around you. He had spent a lot of time alone as a child owing to
a disability that he had overcome, and you could see the pain he
had suffered in his eyes sometimes. He had visited our diocesan
mission in El Salvador and was deeply committed to helping the
poor. He was devoted, too, to his mother, who was often there
when he said Mass. Both his mom and dad helped out in the
kitchen during the Lenten fish fries held in the basement.

There was nothing razzle-dazzle about Father Dan. That was
his greatest strength. He was a good, gentle, dedicated priest
with a deep belief in God and in his vocation: In twenty years as
a priest, not once had he overslept a Mass, not once had he even
been late. Because of the paucity of priests, he would have no
help (no assistants) at Holy Angels. He'd have to say five Masses
during the week, one on Saturday, three on Sunday, plus weddings, baptisms, and funerals. This schedule, some parishioners
feared, would kill this gentle, diminutive man, but Father Dan
never complained. He soldiered on for God.

The parishioners, me included, fell in love with him, with his
self-deprecating sense of humor. He was the most unassuming

man. On those extremely rare occasions when someone else—a visiting missionary hustling up donations—said Mass, Father Dan stood with the choir and sang. He liked to sing. There was no doubt that Father Dan one-upped Father Bob there. While Father Bob's voice was pretty much a bovine bellow, Father Dan's voice was a gift from God.

Those of us parishioners who liked Father Dan very much were rankled by the fact that he couldn't officially be our pastor; he was our "parish administrator," just as Father Bob had been after Father Joe's departure for a gardening career in Florida. Being "parish administrator" and not "pastor" meant a diminishment in prestige. The reason was that the Vatican was still reviewing Father Joe's case—and until Father Joe was officially tossed out, and defrocked, Father Dan could only be an administrator. Some Vatican reviews, we were told, took *fifteen years!* But none of it seemed to matter an iota to Father Dan, who soldiered on no matter his rank or pay.

This is what Father Dan wrote in the church bulletin:

"Last week I attended a conference on Stewardship. . . . One of the workshops I attended was 'Stewardship and Deepening Spirituality in the Parish.' It spoke about the four characteristics of a good steward. These were so powerful I wanted to share them with you. We must be grateful. We should also be responsible. We are called to be generous. God has blessed us with good purpose. Each one of us has something to give—if only a smile, a kindness, an hour of work, a note of support, or a promise of prayers. Lastly, we are challenged to make a return to the Lord with increase. God will ask us: 'What did you do with your life? How did you use the gifts, the talents, and the abilities I gave you?' The Blessed Mother is an example of the perfect steward. She received the word of God *gratefully*. She nurtured the gift *responsibly* by taking care of the child in her womb. She *generously* shared the gift of her Son with the world and then she *returned* to the Father the gift she had been given through the gift of the Cross."

I thought that Father Dan would be a perfect steward for our little church. He was grateful, responsible, and generous of spirit and had in his priesthood always tried to return the Lord's blessings in abundance.

And he obviously loved the Blessed Virgin Mary, which made Naomi like him right away.

Naomi and I trekked across town to Father Bob's installation as pastor at his new parish. I even wore my black Bob Dylan western-swing blazer for the occasion. We felt sorry for Father Bob. His new church was a windowless relic from the seventies that looked more like a timeworn ballroom at the Ramada Inn than a church. And Father Bob told us that the parish was grounded so heavily in the past that it didn't even have any computers. Everything was on paper, and the parish had a venerable fleet of pampered old typewriters! I immediately put in a request for several of the old beauties.

Naomi and I would miss Father Bob, and I would always be indebted to him for his help through a desolate time, but we looked forward to getting to know Father Dan and were soon planning to take him out to lunch.

Sushi. Father Dan, it turned out, *loved* sushi. He also liked going off on cruises where he was the chaplain and took trips to cool places like Palm Springs and Oregon and Alaska. We sensed that we'd have a lot of fun with him.

I HAD PROMISED GOD that I would try to live like a good Christian. My resolve was quickly put to the test one afternoon when, half-asleep in our bedroom, I noticed a man in a car at the end of our driveway taking pictures of the boys, who were playing there.

I couldn't yell to the boys to tell them to get away from whoever that was because I had no voice. I blew a police whistle that I kept around my neck, and when Naomi came running, I pointed to the car at the end of the driveway with the boys.

As we watched, the car started coming down the driveway toward our house. The man driving it had a camera in his hand and was taking pictures of the house now.

I struggled out of bed and stumbled down the stairs, my trache tube wobbling around in my throat. I was trembling. My knees were shaking. I almost fell several times.

I ran out the front door to the driveway. My hair was un-combed. I was bare-chested, red-faced, and wild-eyed. I ran up to the car. The driver was still calmly snapping pictures.

I leaned through his open window and tried to grab his camera.

"What the eff?" the guy said. "What the eff is wrong with you?"

"What the eff are you taking pictures of my kids and house for?" I tried to yell. Nothing came out, of course, except a hiss and some spittle. The driver stared at me, his mouth open, my spittle on his face.

I tried to yell, "Give me that effing camera!" and tried to grab it again.

He jacked his car into reverse, terrified, and stepped on the gas, nearly tearing my arm off as the car swerved down my driveway and out into the street.

We called the cops. They caught him a few streets away. They knew him. He was a real estate photographer taking pictures of recently purchased houses. He hadn't been taking pictures of the kids, only the house.

He told the cops he thought I was a madman who had recently escaped from the loony bin.

I wasn't sure about *that,* but I knew I had certainly just flunked my first Christian behavior test.

I USUALLY WORE JEANS, my Nike LeBrons, and a T-shirt when I carried the cross.

I had a big collection of T-shirts and liked to show them off: Harley T-shirts from Budapest, London, Fairbanks, and even places like El Paso and Muskogee, Oklahoma. I had Michael Jordan T-shirts, LeBron T-shirts, Cleveland Indians T-shirts, and vintage rock-and-roll T-shirts, especially Rolling Stones T-shirts going back to the seventies.

I particularly liked wearing the Stones T-shirts when I carried the cross because I wanted to demonstrate that you didn't have to be some goody-two-shoes twerp to believe in God and love Jesus. I didn't think there was anything uncool, dorky, or nerdy about loving Jesus.

On this particular Sunday, I wore a Stones *Tattoo You* shirt, and I saw a guy glaring at me as I walked back down the aisle, cross in hand, after Mass. He looked like he wanted to kill me. He was about my age, silver-haired and trim. A geezer. He was wearing what looked like a Brooks Brothers suit and rep tie.

He caught up with Naomi and the boys and me in the parking lot. He said his name was Dave and asked if he could speak to me privately a moment. He didn't look like he had a screenplay in his pocket he was peddling, so I said fine and Naomi went to the car with the boys. Dave and I stood there.

He looked me in the eye for a long moment. "How can you wear that T-shirt to church?" he said.

"I like T-shirts. What's the matter with a T-shirt?"

"This particular T-shirt."

I said, "You didn't like *Tattoo You*? I'll wear *Exile on Main Street* next time. What are you, some kind of Beatles freak?"

He looked at me again. His face was turning red.

"Don't you know?" he said. "Mick Jagger is the Antichrist."

"No. *Really?* I didn't know that."

"Well, I'm telling you," he said. He said it nastily.

I said, "Who appointed you the Great Rock Critic in the Sky, friend? I love the Stones. I've always loved the Stones."

"But you've been born again now."

"Bullshit. I'm too old to be born. I've just developed a new relationship with God. What does that have to do with my T-shirt?"

He went into it then. He talked about Altamont and the Satanic vibe the Stones had back then, about "Sympathy for the Devil" and *Their Satanic Majesties Request.* He said the Stones had made a deal with the devil and had replaced their blood at a Swiss clinic, and that was why Mick still scampered around onstage like a sixty-three-year-old teenager. He talked about a Stones video he had seen from the last tour. It was pouring rain, he said, thunder and lightning, and Mick was up onstage, doing "Sympathy," wearing a big hat and a long coat, the lightning flashing all around him, and to Dave that was a moment of sulphurous epiphany. Mick was the Antichrist!

I listened to his prattle and glanced at Naomi and the boys, waiting patiently in the car, and I finally said, "You're completely full of shit, Dave, although you seem to know a helluva lot about the Stones. Tell me the truth, you listen to 'em, don't you?"

"Not anymore," he smirked. "Not now that I know who Mick is."

"The Antichrist."

He nodded.

I said, "Oh boy, Dave, do I feel sorry for you. Everybody knows Mick isn't the Antichrist, everybody knows Keith is."

I grinned. Dave wasn't grinning, though.

"You don't belong here, you should be back in Hollywood. No wonder you wrote *Basic Instinct*."

"You don't know the half of it, I wrote it in thirteen days. And all the time I was writing it, I listened to the Stones. They helped me channel that script from wherever it came from."

He kept gaping at me.

"I'll tell you something else," I said. "In 1994, at a Halloween party in San Francisco during the *Voodoo Lounge* Tour, I met Keith Richards, the Antichrist. He's a very charming Antichrist. He even kissed my wife's hand."

Dave looked at me a long moment and finally said, "I see." He turned and walked away without another word.

A couple of Sundays later, I was dropping Naomi and the boys off before Mass in front of the church. I always drop them off and then park the car.

Just as they were getting out, Dave walked in front of the car on his way into the church.

The car's windows were open, and I suddenly realized I had a Stones CD in the car's stereo. I cranked it up, loud. The first song was "Sympathy for the Devil." It exploded out of the car.

Dave glanced at me and shook his head. And then he started to laugh, still shaking his head.

Moments later, we saw each other inside the sacristy before Mass. I was carrying the cross that day and he was reading the Epistle. We held hands with the altar boys and the deacon as

Father Dan said a prayer. Dave and I squeezed each other's hands at the end of the prayer and grinned at each other.

Father Dan told me after Mass about a husband and wife who had recently joined the parish. They told Father Dan that what had convinced them to join was seeing this no longer young crossbearer wearing a Rolling Stones T-shirt. They said that was the kind of church they wanted to belong to.

"Maybe you should start getting commissions on new membership, like royalties from your movies," Father Dan said with a sly smile.

IF BASEBALL WAS RELIGION, then I was already a passionately religious man. My sons and I had played together all of their lives, and if playing was praying, then we were bound for glory.

I got my baseball religion as a little boy who lied to his parents about going to study at the public library downtown. Instead, I sneaked down to Municipal Stadium and watched the Cleveland Indians lose over and over again.

I played catch a lot, but I mostly played it alone—throwing rubber ball fastballs against the redbrick wall of the Num Num potato chip factory, hitting the pitches as they bounced back, catching them as they came off the wall again.

I asked my dad to play with me, but he, a Hungarian-language novelist, didn't like this American game. Nothing ever happened, he said. The only time my dad took me to a game (as a reward for a good report card), he sat there in his beret and secondhand trench coat reading *Crime and Punishment* as the Indians lost yet another game.

But I kept having a recurring dream that I was playing catch with my father. And as I grew up, I swore that if I ever had sons, I would convert my sons to my private baseball religion and we would see salvation together.

My son Steve was born in 1975, and by the time he was five years old, we were playing catch in the backyard in San Rafael, California. I got him a glove when he was six, and we watched the Oakland A's together each night. And by the time he got to Little League, Steve was a very religious little man. He knew about all the saints: Babe and Joe DiMag and Ted Williams and my own favorite, Bob Feller of the Cleveland Indians.

As Steve and I hunted for holy baseball cards at flea markets and card shows and autograph sessions, I sometimes imagined my father's intellectual, bookish ghost hovering around me, saying: *Why? But why waste time like this?* I knew we weren't wasting time, though, and when Steve and I met my all-time hero, Bob Feller, at a card show, Bob Feller tousled Steve's hair and said, "Play catch with your dad, son, as often as you can. That's how I learned to pitch—by playing catch with mine."

Steve and I played catch all the time, and we watched the Cleveland Indians together whenever they came to town to play the A's. As always, the Indians lost, but I didn't care. I was there with my boy, watching them.

And one day Steve sat down and wrote a letter to Ted Williams, the Splendid Splinter himself, at his home in Florida. Steve wrote about how much he believed in baseball and how much he and I played catch. Steve didn't ask Ted Williams for anything, but at the end of his letter he wrote: "God bless you, Mr. Williams."

I don't know why he finished his letter with those words. Maybe he wrote them because he knew or sensed that he and I and God and the Splinter all shared the same baseball faith.

Maybe he knew that he was saying the same prayers now in Little League that Ted Williams had said his whole life.

At any rate, about a month later, Steve got a letter post-marked from Florida. And when we tore it open, he found a genu-wine 1954 holy card of Ted Williams. And on it the Splinter had signed, "God bless you, too—Ted Williams."

It confirmed for me that Ted—the crusty, boozing, foul-mouthed ex–fighter pilot—was in his heart of hearts a religious man.

My son Joey was born in 1994. My son Nick was born in 1995. My son John Law was born in 1997. My son Luke was born in 2000. Oh, my good Lord, all these many sons to pray and play with! I felt like a missionary of the diamond, a knight of the cross with a Louisville Slugger for my sword. With so many sons to convert, I prayed and played all the time, from morning till night, passionately invoking the saints of baseball—the Babe and DiMag and the Mick and the Splinter—but especially Bob Feller.

Joey was a natural-born hitter with the kind of soulful swing all his Little League coaches admired. Nick was a scrappy little in-fielder who liked getting dirty shagging ground balls and made plays with the fluidity of a Major Leaguer. John Law could run faster than any kid in his class. Luke had such a strong arm at such a tender age that his big brothers all backed up the instant he got his little ham-hock hands on a ball.

So I did what I had done alone as a kid, but this time with my gang of sons. I pitched to them and caught them and stum-bled around like a middle-aged man chasing the butterflies that were their fly balls.

I was in a state of rapture.

Days after I got out of the hospital after my throat surgery,

I told my sons (Steve had flown in from Oregon) that we were going to go out and play ball. All my sons and Naomi argued with me and told me that I was nuts. I still had the trache tube stuck in my throat, and I was weak and fragile from my lengthy hospital stay and my forty-pound weight loss. I said I was going to go out and *pray,* and to hell with them if they weren't coming.

So my sons came out to a nearby diamond at Gardner Elementary School with me, and so did Naomi, who loves me and knew how much this particularly religious moment meant to me. She was the catcher. Steve and Nick spread out around the red-dirt field. John Law played with some ants. Luke sucked on a Gummi Bear. I stood on the mound and pitched to Joey.

On the very first pitch, Joey hit a wicked line drive right back at me. It missed my head only because I snapped my neck back viciously . . . and coughed my trache out on the pitcher's mound.

*No big deal!* Naomi put it back in.

I kept pitching. My sons kept hitting. The sun went down. We went home saved.

Whenever I got scared about my cancer, all I had to do was go outside and play catch with my sons. I thanked the Lord . . . and Babe and the Splinter and DiMag and Bob Feller of the Cleveland Indians. These archangels of the game had interceded on my behalf, and thanks to them, I could still hear the life-affirming *thwack* of cowhide landing in a well-oiled glove.

*Fathers, play catch with your sons, and you shall be . . . born again and again and again and again.*

WE WENT to a lot of Indians ball games and street fairs and carnivals.

"I was swinging out over the lake, my hair flying. I was over-joyed that we were together again. I said, 'What?' I thought it was some juicy bit of neighborhood gossip.

"Dana said, 'I got saved.'

"I said, 'In Sites Lake?' I thought she'd gone out too far and almost drowned.

"She said, 'No. In Alabama. We went to a revival. I saw this preacher. And he told us to ask the Lord to come into our hearts. I did. And the Lord came into my heart.'

"And then Dana said, 'If you don't do the same thing, you're going to burn in hell forever!'

"I said, 'What?' I said, *'What did you say?'* I couldn't believe what she'd said to me.

"And Dana said, 'What we do—kissing each other—it's evil.'

"I said, 'No, it's not.'

"She said, 'Yes, it is. And I'm never going to do it again.'

"She had stopped pushing me, and I was drifting in circles on the swing. I didn't look at her, but I said, 'It's not evil.'

"She said, 'Yes, it is. Oh yes, it is.'

"I got off the swing, got on my bike, and headed for home. I looked back once and saw Dana standing by the empty swing, looking at me. I knew in my heart that nothing would ever be the same again. I have loved God my whole life, but after that moment, nothing ever *was* the same again."

NAOMI had always had a special devotion to the Blessed Virgin Mary, too.

"My faith in the Virgin Mary was sealed when I was ten years old," she told me. "It was my Confirmation Day, and that morning my parents gave me a present: a sterling silver cross necklace with a pearl at its center. We were poor and it was the most expensive thing I'd ever owned, far beyond what my parents could afford. It instantly became my prized possession.

"When we got home from church on my Confirmation Day, there was a party. All the family had gathered to celebrate my big day. The adults sipped their highballs and the other kids went out to play in the yard. My mom said if I changed my clothes, I could join them.

"An hour later my mom called me back in from outside. She wanted me to show off my beautiful cross. I reached for it around my neck. It wasn't there. 'It's upstairs,' I said, and raced past my mom. I was panicked, my heart pounding. My beautiful cross was gone! Lost already, and after only a few hours! I started frantically searching for it. First upstairs, then outside, trying to retrace each step since we got home. In my frenzy I passed my mom again. She said, 'Naomi! Come show Aunt Bernice your cross!'

"I was exhausted. Tears were in my eyes. I ran into my room, closed the door, and started pacing around my bed. Finally I knelt down to pray. Beside my bed on my nightstand was a statue of the Blessed Virgin given to my mom by my grandmother. I knelt down before the Virgin, my hands folded, trembling. I closed my eyes and prayed with all my heart to please please please let me find my cross necklace.

"When I opened my eyes they were blurred with tears, but as I looked at the Virgin I saw my cross. It was hanging from her neck; her face seemed to be gazing down on it. In my excitement I had completely forgotten that I put it there for safekeeping when I changed clothes."

For the rest of her life, whenever something good happened, Naomi said, singsonging the words, "Thank . . . you . . . Blessed . . . Virgin."

When I woke from my throat surgery in the recovery room

and it was clear to Naomi and my son Steve and daughter Suzi that I'd survived, the first thing I heard was, "Thank . . . you . . . Blessed . . . Virgin."

And now, at the end of each day, another day that I had managed to live without cigarettes and alcohol, Naomi said, "Thank . . . you . . . Blessed . . . Virgin."

I AWOKE at four in the morning. I was terrified. I had good reason to be. I was in remission from my cancer, but I was terrified that it would come back.

I asked God to give me more time. To let me live longer.

I was still praying when dawn broke. I watched Joey from our bedroom window. He got on his school bus at seven o'clock. Then Nick got the newspapers from the driveway. Then John Law took the puppy out. Then Lukey cried downstairs because he had to shut off *SpongeBob* and eat. At eight I watched Nick and John Law catch their school bus. The day brightened. The sun began to shine.

I fell back to sleep for an hour or so, still praying but more hopeful now. My heart had brightened along with the day.

THE COYOTE CAFÉ, the roadhouse bar near our house, was a great temptation to me.

Naomi and I had hung out there a couple of times before I stopped drinking. It had sawdust on the floor, lots of different tequilas, a jukebox filled with Ernest Tubb and Toby Keith and Flaco Jiménez and Jerry Lee Lewis singing "The Beer That Made Milwaukee Famous."

The longer and longer I hadn't had a drink, the more and more I thought about the Coyote Café.

Then, one day the Coyote Café burned to the ground.

Which meant to me that once God saves you, if you treat Him right, He might save you in all kinds of other ways as well.

Because sure as hell there was no sense thinking about drinking an ice cold Corona beer in a shit-kicking roadhouse that had been wiped off the face of God's earth.

NOW THAT I BELIEVED in God, I wondered if my throat cancer was punishment for something that I had said.

I had said many ugly, hurtful things to my fellow human beings (all God's children) through the years.

I remembered some of them all too well.

The film director I'd worked with whom I'd called "a doddering old eff" to his face.

The boardroom meeting with fifty people at Walt Disney— *Walt Disney!*—I'd told to "get your hands off my dick!"

The woman I was having an affair with who called me when she got home from my hotel to say, "I can still smell you." And I said to her: "Take a shower."

My ex-wife, who asked me what she should do as our marriage was breaking up. I said, "Get a good lawyer."

The famous stuntman whom I'd called "the King of the Goons" in a magazine piece.

The president of the United States, whom I'd gifted with a talking penis named Willard in a book I'd written.

And all my children, whom I adored and affectionately called "moron" and "idiot" and "dum-dum" and "numb nuts" and "dumbass."

"What did you do—fall on your head?" was something I'd said to both of my wives on several regrettable occasions.

I'd wounded hundreds of my fellow human beings with thousands of eff-bombs and guided missile eff-rockets. And as far as God and Jesus were concerned, I had used Their names thousands of times in anger, usually embellished with colorful (and off-color) renderings that I didn't even want to think about anymore.

A woman at a screening, I remembered, had seen the first ten minutes of *Jagged Edge* and had gone running from the screening room, yelling, "Where's the drunken sailor who wrote this foul piece of shit?"

And I had stopped her and said, "Right effing here!"

Was it possible that I had finally strained God's endless patience? That He had finally said, "Enough already!"

"You—dimwit! You with the big fat loud blasphemous and obscene mouth, let's see how you feel when you can't speak anymore. When no one can understand the croaking gibberish that comes out of your mouth!"

Had I brought this whole horror show upon myself?

Was this my just and deserved karma?

I knew a Hollywood mogul who killed a man and stole his wife and fortune and got away with it. One day years later he was lying down on a Caribbean beach and someone on a construction crane behind him dropped an iron rod. It went straight through the mogul's heart.

*God had put a stake through his heart!*

And I knew a movie star who had sex with at least two women every day and brutally dumped and abandoned all of them. He got cancer of the scrotum; the doctors had to remove his testicles.

*God had cut his balls off!*

Was it possible, then, that *God had cut my throat?*

For a year after my throat surgery, I couldn't speak well enough to be understood clearly. I carried my toy slate blackboard around with me so I could communicate.

I had terrible handwriting, though, so I couldn't "speak" very well.

People couldn't hear me to understand me, and people couldn't read my handwriting, either.

I was in a real box. I had never wanted to rewrite my scripts in Hollywood, and now I was constantly rewriting my toy blackboard in Cleveland. Just so people could make some sense of what I was trying to tell them.

I told God that the biggest reason I wanted my voice back was to sing His praise and glory in church. I had never done that. I had never raised my voice in song to Him.

Now, mute, the quiet man, the dumb man, I wanted to sing.

Over the next year, I was gradually granted a voice. It wasn't my old voice. It was at first a whimper, then a rasp, then a whisper, then a raspy croak, then a croak that was scary but loud enough to be heard.

I croaked His praise and glory each Sunday. I croaked, "Holy God, we praise Thy name," and I croaked, "You are holy, You are mighty," and I croaked, "Lord, I ask You for courage; Lord, I ask You for strength, be with me now, be with me."

Naomi and the boys smiled as I croaked. Adults said, "God bless." Little kids stared and bolted in fright.

A YEAR OR SO AFTER my surgery, as I was sitting in my office in front of my typewriter, staring at it, not writing . . .

my fingers, as though on their own, moved to the keyboard and started typing.

"This is how I found God," my fingers wrote—words that would become the first words of this book.

I kept writing that day and on the days afterward. I no longer needed my cigarettes or my white wine or cognac-laced coffee.

My fingers were just fine now, thank you, sometimes moving almost on their own, as though some other force were controlling them.

I WALKED five miles every day—*every* day—when it was ninety degrees outside and when it was zero. I had become addicted to walking.

I walked in the neighborhood around my house, among towering oaks and elms, down cul-de-sac lanes where families of raccoons populated the ditches. I kept seeing a reddish brown fox in the woods, frozen and wide-eyed, attuned to my every move. I prayed as I walked.

I usually walked at four in the afternoon so I could run into Jack. Jack was eighty-four years old. He was Jewish. He drove around all day and drove by our neighborhood at that hour. Jack had been a contractor all his life, and now that he was retired, he spent his days looking at the houses that he'd built through the course of his long life. Lots of houses. Thousands of houses—including ours.

He drove by each house that he'd built and noted the shape that it was in. And he stopped his car, rolled his window down, and chatted with people like me. He told me once that his houses were his children.

He carried lemon drops with him and gave me some when he stopped to chat. I thanked him and told him how much the boys loved lemon drops, even though they didn't.

Jack stopped and we talked about the weather and the raccoons and the hawk and the blue heron, and Jack said, "You all right?" because he knew about my cancer, and I said, "Yeah, fine," and he gave me the lemon drops, and I thanked him. I said, "See you tomorrow," and then Jack drove off and I saw him tomorrow.

My daily walks were my daily Mass. Jack was the Jewish priest who prayed with me. And Jack's lemon drops, which I sucked on all the way home, were the body of Christ that God had blessed me with.

WHEN I WENT BACK to Hollywood for the first time after I found God, I sat down with the people I'd treated uncharitably through the years and apologized to them for my behavior. I asked them to forgive me for my actions and words.

They listened intently and told me not to worry about it. People say things they don't mean, they said. People behave badly when they're under too much stress, they said. There was nothing to forgive. They asked me how I was feeling and told me, over and over again, that I looked great. I smiled and said that being on intravenous food for almost two weeks was a great diet. They thought that was very funny. They told me my voice sounded great, too, although I knew that my voice was still a croak that could barely be heard.

Many of those to whom I apologized couldn't keep their eyes off the thin silver crucifix I wore on the chain around my neck. They said nothing about it but couldn't stop looking at it.

I felt good about apologizing to everyone and went back home to Ohio feeling that a burden had been lifted off my shoulders.

One of my agents called me a week later and said, "Did you tell everybody you're born again?"

"I am not born again," I said, "I have a new relationship with God."

"Got ya," he said.

"What if they *do* think I'm born again, so what?"

"So what? They'll think you've lost your mind, that's what."

"I'm sorry," I said, "but I had to apologize. It's part of my new relationship with God."

"You don't get it. Being born again is much worse as far as they're concerned than whatever abusive thing you may have said or done to them in the past. That kind of abuse happens in this industry all the time. That doesn't need their forgiveness. Some people even like that. It's an indication of passion and commitment. But being born again—they'll never forgive you for that."

"I told you, I'm not born again, but I have a new relation-ship—"

"Fine. Whatever. But tell me this—did you really wear a cross in the bar of the Four Seasons?"

"Everybody wears a cross. Don King, P. Diddy, even Keith Richards wears a cross. And he's the Antichrist."

"He is?"

"Yup."

"Oh," he said. He thought about it. "I see. You're right. So the cross doesn't have any real meaning for you. It's just hip jewelry."

"Bullshit," I said. "No, it's *not* just jewelry. It's the symbol of Christ's suffering and redemption. It means everything to me.

It's getting me through my recovery. If you want to know the truth, sometimes I even wear a rosary around my neck."

"That's all right," he said. "I saw them selling those beads in gold and silver at Dolce and Gabbana. I get it, now. The cross you wear is part of your illness. It's like taking medicine. You take it for a while and then you stop."

"No," I said. "The cross will give me strength till the day I die. I will always wear one."

There was a long pause, then the agent said, "Joe, you know I love ya. I do. I really do. I'm going to give you some advice from my heart. You need some help, dude. Some therapy, dawg. Somebody to help you work your way through this shit. You've been traumatized, that's all. The cancer, getting off the booze and the cigarettes, losing your voice, and not being able to communicate must have been a diminishing experience—and all of that was on top of your divorce and *Showgirls* and *Jade* both disastering and you moving back to Ohio, of all places. If all of that isn't traumatizing, I don't know what is. The same thing happened to Dylan, remember that motorcycle accident, the records not selling—he got born again for a while. Then he got some good help, now he's a good Jewish boy again. No more Jesus. Back out on the road doing his gigs, making money. You get yourself worked through this by somebody good, then we'll pull down some big seven-figure bank heists again. But meanwhile, you've got to stop talking about this Jesus thing. Take my advice, okay?"

I told him I'd think about it, and I did.

I fired him the next day.

Then *he* told everybody in the industry that I was crazy, that I'd lost my mind. It gave everybody a good laugh.

From *Basic Instinct* and *Showgirls* to wearing a cross at the bar of the Four Seasons. From having a big and nasty mouth to having a croak of a voice that could barely be heard. From threats to apologies. From Malibu to Ohio. From booze to Diet Sprite. From Spago to McDonald's. From Sharon Stone to Jesus. They laughed and laughed.

I HAVE FOUND GOD, I told my son Steve.

Steve was thirty-one years old. He was one of my best friends. He'd never believed in God.

Steve looked at me curiously, seriously, assessingly. And I saw it in his eyes: "Has Pops lost his marbles?"

Steve smiled, looked at me. "Pops," he said, "I'm happy for you. Maybe it will happen to me someday, too. Who knows?"

The year after I told him about me and God, Steve came to visit for Thanksgiving. I asked if he wanted to come to church with me Thanksgiving morning; Naomi and the boys were involved with the turkey and with making this a perfect day. Steve said of course he'd come with me. I knew he didn't want Pops to have to go to church alone.

It had snowed overnight. It was still snowing. The world was a white sheet.

It snowed during Mass. The walls of our church were windows, and the walls were a kaleidoscope of swirling snowflakes. God had kissed the day.

I held Steve's hand at the Our Father. Steve said the words with me, staring at the whiteout beyond the glass.

We spent most of the ride home in silence. Steve said, "This is really beautiful." He seemed awed.

That night, Thanksgiving night, Steve hugged me good night and said, "Thank you, Pops, for this morning."

I would so much like to say that my son Steve, through me, found God. But no. This past Halloween he decked himself out as Father Karras from *The Exorcist*—wearing cross and reverenda. Steve's fiancée dressed as Linda Blair. She wore a white nightgown with fake vomit on it.

Every Thanksgiving, as Steve's visit approaches, I ask God to provide us with another spectacular snowfall that will awe my son's soul.

But God sends us rain or sunshine, unseasonably hot weather. Steve is not awed.

That's okay. I get it. I know God enjoys playing His little games, busting my chops.


I WAS TELLING EVERYONE that I had found God for the same reason I had told my friends in 1997 that I had seen a UFO.

There were hundreds of millions of people out there who didn't believe either in God or in UFOs, and I believed it to be the responsibility of those who had experienced God (or UFOs) to say, "I'm a witness!" to all those people.

God exists. UFOs exist. God was in my heart, and I had seen a UFO with my own eyes on a spring night in 1997 in Malibu.

I had woken up with an uneasy, frightened feeling at two in the morning. As soon as I woke up, I had reached into my nightstand and pulled out a two-shot .45 magnum Derringer that I kept in the drawer. Then, gun in hand, I had rolled over and seen the most spectacular light show I'd ever seen— multicolored lights swirling around in the sky above the sea and the bluffs along the shore.

I tried to get Naomi up, but she couldn't hear me. She had inserted earplugs because I snored deafeningly. I stepped out on our bedroom patio, which overlooked the Pacific Ocean. I was naked and waving the gun around with my hand. The light show was taking place all around me. And then, right above the beach, there was a spacecraft with bright lights on the bottom of it. It looked very much like Spielberg's spacecraft in *Close Encounters of the Third Kind*. And suddenly a blindingly bright stream of light came blazing from the bottom of the craft straight toward the beach. It was so bright the sand radiated, and after a few seconds, the craft *swooshe*d soundlessly high into the sky—faster than any airplane—toward Santa Monica.

Everything was still. The light show was over.

I had no doubt that I had seen a UFO. And because I had always scoffed at the existence of UFOs, I told everyone now what I had seen. Some people nodded knowingly. Others looked at me like I was nuts.

I apologized to Steve. For years Steve had been trying to convince me about the existence of UFOs. He had read every book on the subject. And for years I had been making fun of him and laughing at him. Now I called him and apologized. Now I called myself a stubborn, mule-headed, aging A-hole. Now I knew that UFOs exist and that I had been wrong. Because now I had seen one.

And now I knew, too, that God exists. Because I felt Him in my heart. Because I had asked for His help and He had given it to me. Because He had given me the strength to fight my addictions. So I was telling everyone I knew that God exists. Some nodded knowingly and smiled. Others looked at me like I was nuts.

I could hear what they were saying: "This guy is so out there that he not only goes on and on about God, but he also goes on and on about light shows and UFOs. Maybe he smoked some bad weed sometime."

I didn't care what anyone said. I wasn't going to lie about it. Nor was I going to stay quiet about it. *I was a witness!* I was *excited* to tell the truth about what I had seen and witnessed.

I saw a UFO, and I personally experienced God's grace. And I never smoked any bad weed. I only smoked the finest weed money could buy . . . and that was a long time ago.

ALTHOUGH I had been saved and the church I attended was called Holy Angels, and although I even believed in UFOs, I still couldn't convince myself to believe in angels.

For the sake of my children, I believed in unicorns and tooth fairies and Santa, but *angels*? Or, as they sang the word in my church, *ayen-jells*? Those mighty bird-creatures fluttering high up there in the sky—*it's a bird, it's a plane, it's a holy ayen-jell!* Ayen-jells who sometimes waved swords in their hands, as the Bible prophesied. Murderous, homicidal, apocalyptic angels? Kewpie doll, cutesy-poo do-gooder angels? Or snarky John Travolta angels? Or rum-dum, pass-the-bottle Frank Capra angels out of *It's a Wonderful Life*? May God forgive me, but I couldn't buy into any of it. It all felt like cheesy science fiction. The flapping of angelic wings sounded too hokey to me.

When I was a boy, my mother tried to convince me to pray to my guardian angel each night. I believed then that something watched over me, but I thought it was God. I didn't understand how a dumb, wing-flapping angel had cut in on God's action. Believing in angels, guardian or otherwise, I sensed even then, was two tokes over the line, sweet Jesus.

If you were Catholic, then you had to believe in God the Father, God the Son, Jesus, and God the Holy Spirit. Plus the Blessed Virgin Mary—"the BVM," the nuns had called her—a huge gaggle of all kinds of saints from all over the world . . . and then the angels. It was *a lot* to have to believe in, and I didn't seem to have the time, energy, or inclination even then (we didn't much believe in fairy tales in the part of town where I grew up) to extend my belief to angels.

The fact that I was Hungarian born was probably one reason I had such a hard time believing. According to Hungarian tradition, it was the angel who brought the Christmas tree each year (as baby Jesus brought gifts). But I quickly realized that our Christmas angel had something personal against me. We got such a bare-ass, ugly-looking, scrawny little tree each year that there was no other explanation. Some years the only decorations on the tree were Hungarian candies wrapped in newspaper and colored pages from magazines tied into little bows and placed on the tree's limbs. I saw some of the other Christmas trees that the Christmas angel brought for my friends—big, wondrous trees with multicolored, sometimes even bubbling lights —and I thought: Some angel you are! What could I possibly have done to deserve this plug-ugly tree with trash and rock-hard candy on it?

There was another Hungarian Christmas tradition that called for a good angel and a bad angel to show up on December 6 and determine whether you'd been good or bad all year. This was a very big deal in the refugee camps where I spent my first six years. The kids were all herded together when it got dark that day, and here came the angels—shrieking and flapping their wings. One angel was dressed in white and the other in black and had red horns on his head. I started to cry as soon as I heard the faintest flap of their wings. Both the good angel and the bad angel scared me to death. I couldn't understand then what I could possibly have done that was *that* bad—to deserve these scary, shrieking fiends. I lived in a barracks and I played among soldiers and I ate pine needle soup and rotted horse cadaver stew. And those shrieking freakish angels were arguing about whether I'd been *good or bad* all year?

When I got a little older, I went to Hungarian catechism

class at Saint Emeric's School in Cleveland and learned that the devil himself, whom we called *"shawton,"* had once been an angel, too, named Lucifer. I tried to envision the megagalactic war between the angels that we heard about in catechism—between Lucifer and Michael and Gabriel and the other good guys—but I somehow couldn't buy into that, either. Up there high in the sky, Lucifer and Michael and Gabriel and the good guys, flapping their wings menacingly at one another and flashing their comic-book swords. All my young but developing shit detectors went off.

For a while in catechism class, I tried to figure out how the whole guardian angel industry worked. On what basis did God assign an angel to his or her task? Were there male and female angels? Did male angels get male clients, or did it matter? Did those dead humans who for some reason wound up in limbo get drafted to be guardian angels? If the client the guardian angel watched over died, could the angel retire, or was he or she reassigned? If they were reassigned, did they have to spend eternity working? (This didn't seem fair, either.) And when a client died or got sick, did it mean that the angel screwed up? Or did God order his or her death or illness? Did it mean, for example, that my mom got schizophrenia because her angel fell asleep one day? Got distracted? Was flirting with another angel?

I thought now . . . as a man in his sixties sitting in a pew at Holy Angels Church . . . about that boy in catechism class who'd tried his best to figure out the guardian angel industry. While there was no doubt now that the child had been father to the man, I also wanted to say to that boy: *Dude, the things you were worried about! Mom's schizophrenia was because of her guardian angel?!*

But I had seen something in the papers recently that disturbed me. The Catholic Church officially announced that there was no limbo anymore. No limbo? *Say what, Willis?* All these years we'd heard about limbo, where guardian angels (and dead infants) lived. Now suddenly there was no limbo anymore? Then where were all the guardian angels living now?

Had they been deported to purgatory, maybe? That wouldn't have been fair, either—we'd learned in catechism class that it was sizzling hot in purgatory (a halfway house between heaven and hell), though certainly not as hot as in hell. If the guardian angels were now in purgatory, did it mean that they deserved to sizzle a little?

I wasn't going to worry about it, though. I just sang the songs about the holy angels I didn't believe in.

BOBBY was my brother-in-law from my first marriage. I met him when he was sixteen years old—eight years younger than me. He was a shy, fiery, good-looking kid.

We became best friends. We played basketball together, we shot pool together till five in the morning, we went to a bunch of Indians games at the old Municipal Stadium down on the lakefront in Cleveland. I felt like I was Bobby's big brother.

He was especially shy, I quickly realized, about girls and sex. His mother still inspected his sheets for telltale spots each morning. His father talked a lot about how long-suffering Saint Joseph had been, and he kept saying about himself, "The dog will have his day." His father was a stone alcoholic who drank a fifth of vodka each night, beginning the moment he got home from work at four thirty in the afternoon. The bottle was a dead soldier by nine o'clock.

A pretty girl lived a few doors down the street from Bobby in another house right on Lake Erie, and she kept letting him know that she liked him. But Bobby wasn't interested. I thought he was interested—very interested—but was so shy that he couldn't act it out.

I moved to California with his sister, Gerri, and didn't see Bobby for a couple of years—until he decided to drive across America and stopped off to see us in Mill Valley. He had found God. He had started reading the Bible, he said, and now he couldn't put the Good Book down. He talked to me about Jesus and His crucifixion and what His resurrection meant to the world.

"He saved you, Joe," he said to me. "He died for you."

I wasn't interested in talking about God or Jesus. I asked him if he had any girlfriends. He shook his head. I asked him if he was still a virgin, and he said shyly, "Yup. Probably always will be, too," and laughed. He started talking about Jesus again. I didn't want to talk about Jesus anymore. I wanted to talk about sex, but Bobby wasn't interested.

He left. He was driving up the Oregon coastline, he said, and would stop off to see us again in Mill Valley on his way back to Ohio.

He was back in six weeks. It was clear to Gerri and me that something traumatic had happened to him. He was vacant-eyed and unkempt. He had lost twenty pounds and had no appetite. He sat on our living room couch for hours, staring at nothing, saying nothing. I saw him in our spare bedroom one night kneeling, his hands clasped in prayer, his rosary in his hands.

I took him for a long walk the next day and spoke to him like a big brother. I loved him, I said. I couldn't stand to see him like this. Something was very wrong. What was it? Bobby denied at first that anything was wrong, but after I kept pressing him, telling him that he was my little brother, he started to cry. We sat on a bench near the top of Mt. Tam, and he haltingly told me his story.

He had driven up the Oregon coast from our house and stopped at a small seacoast town. He had gotten a job as a dishwasher at a resort hotel—a couple hundred bucks a week plus room and board at an annex next to the hotel.

He had met a girl there, a waitress who also worked at the hotel and lived in the annex. She was a beautiful girl, Bobby said, the prettiest girl there, and she liked him. They had fun kidding around and talking. They went out drinking at a local bar and afterward she asked him to her room, and for the first time in his life Bobby had sex. He didn't call it "having sex" to me. "We made love," Bobby said. He smoked a joint with her (which he'd also never done), and they had sex three more times.

And they woke up on a gloriously spectacular morning in a room by the sea and Bobby asked her to marry him. He told her he loved her and would always love her. He told her she was the best thing that had ever happened to him. In his whole life. And he told her the Bible said that having sex without being married was a sin. So they had to stop sinning and get married.

The girl stared at him, Bobby said, and then she said to him—word for word—Bobby would never forget, he said, her exact words: "Oh, my God, what the eff is wrong with you? You're effing crazy, aren't you?" She started to laugh then and she said, "Get the eff out of my room, you sick eff."

That night in the kitchen of the hotel, Bobby saw the girl whispering with another guy who worked there. They whispered together, looked at him, and then they both started laughing at him.

The next morning Bobby proposed to the girl again, and this time she said, "If you don't leave me alone, I'm going to get you fired!" Then she called him "a whacko." Bobby watched the girl for the next few days as she flirted with other guys. He spied on her as she took other guys into her room at night. He smelled the marijuana that drifted into the corridor from under her door.

He couldn't take it anymore. He started hearing voices in his head. One voice was Jesus. Jesus said: "You have to marry her. You made love with her. Tell her you love her. Redeem your sin." The other voice was Satan. Satan said, "Take her clothes off. Tell her you want to eff her. She wants to eff you. *Eff her, eff her, eff her.*"

The voices wouldn't let Bobby sleep or concentrate on anything. Jesus's voice was loud and hard, a voice from the Old Testament. Satan's voice was screeching and wailing, a voice from hell.

Bobby gathered his things and jumped in his car and drove, headed for our house in Mill Valley. But he stopped at the first town he got to, overpowered by a sudden urge to see a priest. It was Jesus telling him: "See a priest, Robert, he'll help you." Bobby said Jesus never called him Bobby, always Robert. Satan called him "effhead" or "scumbag" or some other degrading name.

Bobby found a Catholic church and a rectory next to it and knocked on the door. A priest answered. He was in his late fifties, early sixties. He wore a T-shirt and jeans.

Bobby told him he needed to speak to him right away. He had to make his confession right away. The priest asked him into the house and sat Bobby down on the living room couch. He heard Bobby's confession. There was a simple wooden crucifix above the couch.

Bobby confessed to having had sex with the beautiful girl at the hotel, and he told the priest that he had asked the girl to marry him right away but she had refused. The priest forgave Bobby his sin and said the girl was a "harlot—evil, Satan's pawn."

The priest said Bobby had to renounce Satan from now on and had to be on constant lookout for "Satan's pawns." The priest held Bobby's hands in that rectory living room as the sun went down and said the rosary with him.

When they finished the rosary, the priest asked Bobby if he wanted to have dinner at the rectory with him. Bobby agreed. They ate in the kitchen—TV dinners. The priest opened a bottle of wine. They shared it. He opened another. They shared that, too.

They moved back to the living room. The priest asked Bobby about his sexual experiences. Bobby told the truth, that except for the beautiful girl at the hotel, he'd had no sexual experience. The priest asked him if he masturbated. Bobby told him the truth again—that he tried not to, but he couldn't help it. The priest said he mustn't. Masturbation was a mortal sin.

The priest said maybe the problem was that Bobby didn't like girls. The priest put his hand on Bobby's penis and started rubbing it. The priest said, "Your thingamajig is nice and big."

That's what the priest called it, Bobby said, a "thingamajig."

Bobby jumped off the couch, completely batshit. He heard Satan inside his head laughing like a fiend. He heard Jesus telling him to run for his life. Bobby ran. The priest ran after him. The priest said, "Please, please, Robert, I was just trying to help you." Bobby ran to his car and stomped on the gas pedal.

"I have sex for the first time in my life," Bobby said to me on this trail in Mill Valley. "And it's great. The best thing I've ever felt. So I ask her to marry me and she tells me I'm crazy for wanting to marry her. Then she makes sure I know that she's doing the same thing she did in there with me, but now she's doing it with other guys. And then I need to find someone to talk to and he prays with me and tries to get my *thingamajig* out of my pants. I don't think I'm crazy, but I'm starting to think everybody else in the world is."

He laughed for the first time since he'd come back to us from Oregon. He said, "What the hell kind of dumb A-hole calls it a *thingamajig*?"

I was laughing so hard with him that I could barely talk. I finally said, "You went to the wrong priest for solace, that's for sure," and that made both of us laugh even harder.

Bobby still wasn't eating anything and was losing more weight. He started having migrainelike attacks from what he said were the voices of Jesus and Satan yelling at each other too loudly. He sat sometimes at our kitchen table holding his head, in obvious pain, and said, "Come on, you guys, stop it!" He was talking to Jesus and Satan.

I sent Bobby to my physician, who gave him a physical, found nothing wrong, but sent him to a psychologist. The psychologist studied him for three days and told Bobby he was suffering from schizophrenia. It was not uncommon for schizophrenia to develop in a person's early twenties, the psychologist said.

Bobby went back to Cleveland, to his mother and father's house on the lake. "Pray for me, Joe," he said before he left, and I said I would, although I'm sure he knew I was shining him on. He knew I didn't believe in prayer then. He knew I was just saying that to make him feel better.

His schizophrenia worsened, my mother-in-law told us, after he got back to Cleveland. He was up at all hours of the night, yelling at Jesus and Satan to leave him alone. He had to drop out of community college because their voices blocked everything else out. He stayed in his room most of the time and prayed. He had started to paint. His paintings were mostly of devils and demons. Even his sole painting of Jesus made Him look satanic.

When I spoke to Bobby on the phone, he told me to "stay

away from the harlots in Hollywood." (I thought to myself: How does he know about that? Even his sister didn't seem to know about that.) He told me to pray. "God wants you to pray for the forgiveness of your sins, Joe," he said. "You're a sinner."

He also told me that "the devil is winning the battle for me." He couldn't stop himself, he said, from having "impure thoughts." The devil, he said, was telling him to do again what he had done with the beautiful girl in Oregon. His mother said she had caught him several times playing with his thingamajig.

She called one day, panicked, to tell us that Bobby had locked himself into his room and hadn't come out in three days. He hadn't eaten anything or had anything to drink. She heard him in the room, she said, "yelling terrible things at Jesus."

I knew he badly needed psychiatric help, but he had resisted all of our efforts to hook him up with a psychologist. Bobby didn't trust doctors anymore—he thought they were "in Satan's employ."

A friend of mine in Cleveland suggested that the Free Clinic sometimes got involved in cases like this. I called the Free Clinic and spoke to its director. David was a young and hip man who had heard of me and my films and said that he was happy to help.

He went out to the house by the lake and talked Bobby out of his room. Bobby liked David. He went with him to a psychologist who put Bobby on some powerful medications. The medications did some good. The voices inside his head were still there, Bobby said, but Jesus and Satan weren't yelling and screaming at him anymore. Now they just took their individual turns talking to Bobby, competing for his soul.

Years went by. Bobby stayed on his medications. He put on fifty pounds, then forty more. He became obese. He worked for a while as a deliveryman at a liquor store, then lost his job because of his weight. He stayed home all the time now, painting. His father died of pancreatic cancer (the alcoholic's death), and Bobby became even more religious. He went to Mass every morning. He wore a rosary and two scapulars around his neck. He read the Bible constantly.

He began work on the intricate design of a massive cuckoo clock with the figures of Jesus and the apostles and saints. The figures on the cuckoo clock took turns appearing every fifteen minutes. Bobby sent his blueprints to the Vatican and began to write the pope. Bobby said he would be happy to fly to Rome and begin construction of the clock. It would be at least fifteen stories tall, he wrote, a new Wonder of the World. The pope didn't answer any of Bobby's letters.

And then, for whatever reason, he turned against me. He saw a movie of mine called *Big Shots,* about two little boys, one white and one black, going off on an adventure . . . and said, "It's movies like *Big Shots* which are ruining America." Black people, he decided, were "the devil's helpers." Bobby's mother told us these things because Bobby would speak neither to his sister nor to me. We were demons, Bobby said, and our children were "Satan's spawn."

When *Basic Instinct* was released, he saw a trailer for the movie on television and told his psychologist he was driving to California. To kill me, he said. The psychologist called Gerri and me, panicked, and told us to flee our home. Bobby's mother told us he was gone all right—in the family car, with two hunting rifles. We fled to Hawaii until security people I had hired found him in a jail cell in Mexico City. He'd been busted for vagrancy. My security guys flew him to a psychiatric clinic back in Cleveland.

But nothing changed. More years went by. He had aged so much so suddenly that when people saw him on the street with his mother, they thought they were husband and wife. He still talked about Jesus and Satan inside his head, fighting for him. Sometimes, his mother said, even in public, he dropped to his knees suddenly and started to pray. Satan, Bobby said, was putting impure thoughts inside his head. He still wouldn't speak to us. Gerri and I were still demons, and our children were still "Satan's spawn."

When I divorced Gerri, my now nearly grown kids told me that their uncle Bob had taken a painting of my mother, which we had somehow accidentally left at the house by the lake, and burned it on the beach. My poor schizophrenic mother, I knew, would quickly have forgiven my poor schizophrenic brother-in-law.

I hadn't spoken to Bobby in almost ten years when Naomi and I and our boys moved back to Ohio from California. I thought about Bobby a lot after I found God. I remembered that rosary he wore around his neck when I put my rosary around mine. His mother was dead now. I knew he was living all alone in that big house by the lake. (Months before his mother died, he had beaten her up and spent a weekend in jail.) He was speaking to Gerri again. Now that I'd divorced her, she wasn't a demon anymore, it seemed. He told Gerri that he was going to Mass all the time with a new friend, an old lady with white hair whom he had met in church.

I thought at times about driving over to see him. His house on the lake was no more than an hour away from our new house in Bainbridge Township. If I went to see him, I could tell him that I still loved him, that I thought about him all the time, and that I prayed for him now every day. I thought I could ask him to pray for me. His connection to God was of longer standing than mine.

But I didn't go to see him. I had four more of "Satan's spawn" now, and I didn't want to risk Bobby doing them any harm. Son of Sam, I knew, had heard voices, too. Son of Sam, I remembered, had Satan's voice in his head, too.

One summer day Bobby was found dead in the bathtub of the house by the lake. He had been in that tub for days. The old lady with whom he was going to church had summoned the police. Bobby had suffered a massive heart attack, brought on by the weight, probably, and the stress of Jesus and Satan still screaming at each other inside his brain after all these years.

The police report described him as an obese white man with white hair. He was naked, except for the rosary and the two scapulars around his neck.

I HAD SEEN *The Passion of the Christ* six times. I had never been moved like this by a film before (*The Deer Hunter* and *Field of Dreams* came close), and even though I knew about the innards of moviemaking in all its behind-the-scenes ugliness, this film was like a prayer to me. It made me cry—as had *The Deer Hunter* and *Field of Dreams*—but unlike those two films, this one I kept wanting to see over and over again.

I knew I was probably more moved by it than most because at this particular moment of my life I viewed Christ's suffering as a personal example to me. Recovering from cancer and addictions certainly didn't amount to a crucifixion, but maybe those of us who were fighting cancers and addictions were going through minicrucifixions and were, in our relatively tiny way, the victims of torture and humiliation. Jesus was the way, the truth, and the life, and by His example, He was giving me strength to deal with my own miseries.

I saw the movie first with my Holy Angels Church group at a special screening. I have seen it since in various multiplexes around Cleveland—in neighborhoods rich and poor; once in a predominantly black neighborhood where the theater turned into a Pentecostal church. The air was filled with cries of "Amen!" and "Hallelujah!" and shouted, private testimonies as people munched their popcorn and M&M's. A woman wailed, "Oh, no! No, Lord! Don't do it! Don't do it!" all the way through the film's excruciating crucifixion sequence.

At that initial church screening, I sat next to a young theologian from John Carroll University who, when the film ended, told me that the film seemed to him to be an adaptation of a book called *The Dolorous Passion of Our Lord Jesus Christ* by an eighteenth-century German nun and mystic named Anne Catherine Emmerich.

I rounded up the book from Amazon and read it in the next few days. It read like a dark, spooky, and powerful novel, although Emmerich had claimed it was a transcription of her vision about Jesus's crucifixion, dictated to a German writer. Demons and devils pranced and preened through the book's pages, as they had in Mel Gibson's film. The book seemed to me at times to be a horror novel or a dark graphic comic book in the guise of a sacred document.

My young theologian, I decided, was right. Gibson's film was an adaptation of the book, although Emmerich's book received no screen credit. All of Mel's talk about how the film was adapted from the Bible and the evangelists was bunk—if you read Emmerich's book. The movie was, very simply, a screen depiction of Emmerich's hallucinatory vision.

I thought I knew why Mel never mentioned Emmerich's book and didn't credit the book onscreen. It was because *The Dolorous Passion of Our Lord Jesus Christ,* besides being dark, spooky, and powerful, was also scurrilously and viciously anti-Semitic, filled with descriptions like "the cruel Jews" (p. 81) and "the crime of the Jews" (p. 64) and "the Jews, having exhausted their barbarity . . ." (p. 102).

I imagined, faced with a firestorm of charges that his film was anti-Semitic, Mel Gibson would certainly not want to admit that his film was taken from a transparently vicious anti-Semitic document. So he fudged and said that he had "written" the film with an unknown screenwriter.

I asked myself: Was I so moved, then, by an anti-Semitic screed?

I had spent many years studying the Holocaust; I had even been awarded the Emanuel Foundation's Lifetime Achievement Award for writing about the Holocaust in Hungary. Was it possible that *I* could be manipulated by a piece of anti-Semitism? Did a scurrilous piece of anti-Semitic propaganda make me cry? Was my "prayer" of a film a hateful example of Goebbelsian propaganda? Had I lost some brain cells in the course of my surgery, withdrawal, and ongoing recovery?

But as I watched the film over and over again I decided that, no, I wasn't wrong about *The Passion of the Christ*. Because the *movie itself* wasn't anti-Semitic. Gibson, it seemed to me, had worked very hard as a director to absolve himself of those charges and to strip his film of the anti-Semitism that suffused Emmerich's book. Gibson's lack of anti-Semitism could especially be seen in the screen depiction of Simon of Cyrene, a Jew who helped Jesus carry His cross. Simon was a benign and heroic character, and Gibson made no secret of the fact that he was a Jew.

I didn't know Mel personally, although my good friend Alan, who was Jewish and had lost family members in the Holocaust, was Mel's publicist (as he had been mine). I knew Alan well and respected and admired him and felt sure he wouldn't work so hard for a man who was either anti-Semitic himself or had created something that would fuel the flames of anti-Semitism worldwide. In other words, nothing could convince me that a proud and strong Jew like Alan would put his energy and talent to work on behalf of something that would make people hate . . . *him*. I saw *The Passion of the Christ* for the seventh time and cried again.

Another reason I liked the movie so much was that Jesus was a real man in the film, a tough guy who endured His suffering— His "moment of doubt and pain," as Mick Jagger wrote— heroically.

Mel and Jim Caviezel, who starred as Jesus, had given Jesus *cojones,* a quality lacking in Him in all the simpering depictions onscreen or onstage (except in Willem Dafoe's).

The popular culture had wimpified Jesus. He had been re-duced to a pious, fey, prattling sissy. His manhood had been taken from Him.

Wrongly, of course. The real historical Jesus had thrown a wilding at the Temple and had gone on a vigilante rampage against the thieves and lowlifes hanging around there. And when He faced Satan's temptation in the desert, Jesus hadn't namby-pambied around him, but in nearly Clint Eastwood terms, He had told Satan to eff off and die.

And with His life at stake in His moment with Pilate, Jesus hadn't asked for anything, He hadn't kissed Pilate's rosy red— He'd looked at Pilate with Clint's squint and said, "You know damn well who I am, so let's cut the shit and do what you have to do."

But the media had turned Jesus into a smarmified, cheesy Mr. Rogers. *Jesus is love! Jesus is love! Jesus is love!* the Jesus ex-perts opined on radio and television. And while that was true, it was also true that Jesus got almighty pissed off sometimes, that He was capable of bringing it, and that He could handle having the absolute holy shit beaten out of Him better than anyone, even Rocky Balboa.

NOW THAT I WAS PRAYING, receiving Holy Communion, going to church each Sunday, and carrying the cross, did it mean that I was a Catholic again?

It probably did, I knew, but I was stiffly resisting being one. I had always had serious issues with the Catholic Church. Too much blood had been shed in the effort to convert the heathen hordes of various "dark continents." I was especially angry about the church's complicity in the Holocaust. Eugenio Pacelli, who would become Pope Pius XII, was the papal nuncio to Hitler's Germany and was too close to the Führer for my taste. As pontiff, he did little to stop the Nazis, and many war criminals had gotten away through an elaborate underground railroad managed, mostly, by Franciscan monks.

My own childhood experiences with Hungarian Catholic priests hadn't been very good, either. The priests were anti-Semitic almost to a man and espoused the notion that "the Jews killed Jesus." They were also ugly human beings. My father worked for them at a Hungarian-language Catholic newspaper, so I saw them at unfortunate close range. One Franciscan had sex with a woman linotype operator atop a printing shop table; another got drunk and hit a boy with his car, turning him into a paraplegic; a third stole all the money in the newspaper's bank account and fled back to Hungary with it.

A priest tried to hit on me all the time when I was fourteen years old. Another tried to pick up girls as he drove me to high school. He wore a cowboy hat, his face was plastered with Mantan, and he wolf-whistled the girls from the car at the bus stops.

I had known only two good priests in my childhood. One, Father Steve, threatened to punch out the priest who had been hitting on me if he tried to touch me again. The other, Father John, was a lifelong friend who kept me out of juvenile jail as a boy and whose recommendation helped me get my first job as a journalist. I carried the casket at Father John's funeral and met his longtime mistress and his two daughters. He had an entirely secret other life that no one had known anything about. The mistress/wife and Father John's daughters lived in a city far from Cleveland.

One big reason I resisted viewing myself as a Catholic again was that there was little doubt the Catholic Church had become the pedophile's church. I had four handsome boys, and there were stories in the newspapers every day about how handsome boys like mine had been sexually abused, sometimes on the altar itself, by thousands of priests all over the world. The church hierarchy, it was clear, had covered it up for many years and was still covering it up . . . just like they had covered up their pittypat with the Nazis.

And while the truth was that many priests were gay, the Catholic Church still considered homosexuality a mortal sin and cast gay people into hell for their sins. It was a hypocrisy of mammoth proportions. Women, meanwhile, weren't allowed to become priests solely because of gender prejudice, even though there was increasing evidence that Jesus had women apostles and that Mary Magdalene had been Jesus's chief apostle.

Celibacy was still the rule among Catholic clergy, and that, in my mind, was the basis of the church's problems, the biggest reason there was such a paucity of young priests. It was the biggest reason the Catholic Church was doomed and dying. Celibacy meant that you couldn't be a priest, you couldn't spread the word of God, unless you were a sexual freak, whacking at your thingamajig until hair grew on your palms and you went blind (as the nuns used to tell me).

I wondered how celibate priests had the chutzpah to be marriage counselors, for example. What did they know about male-female intimate life? Knowing full well that they knew *nothing,* how could they then in good conscience dispense advice to men and women and pretend to know about sexual betrayal?

Father Dan, our new pastor, it turned out, did marriage counseling on "Retrovaille Weekends," held at different hotels. Father Dan looked tired on some Sundays during these "Retrovaille Weekends," and I had no doubt that this gentle and compassionate man was doing his best to bring troubled couples back together. But I feared he didn't know what he was talking about—unless he, like my friend Father John, had a wife and a couple of kids stashed somewhere.

I didn't think Father Dan did, but I liked him. I wanted him to follow Father John's example, to praise God and have sex and raise kids—all at the same time.

ABORTION was one of the issues upon which I agreed with Catholic Church teaching. Abortion, except for the victims of rape, was murder. A grievous offense against God and man.

When I was a young man, I had lent two thousand dollars to a friend whose girlfriend was pregnant. He paid for her abortion with my money. Which meant that *I'd* paid for it. He never paid me back, so it was clear that *I* had paid for it. I participated in the murder of another human being. And as an older man, I'd had unprotected sex with a young woman who told me she had already had six abortions. She was a serial killer, but what did I care? I cared only about her body and the

A LOT OF PEOPLE told me that they liked the way I carried the cross.

I carried the cross as though I were actually carrying Jesus. And if you were actually carrying Jesus, the Son of God, you had to carry Him with the respect He deserved.

I had seen crossbearers who chewed gum, who smiled and winked at their friends in the pews, who held the cross crooked, who forgot to pick it up from its stand at the end of the Mass, and who then had to go tripping over themselves to get to the altar. I had seen a crossbearer turn from the altar, cross in hand, and almost knock an altar boy's head off with it. And once I heard a lot of clanking in the church foyer and knew that some fool had dropped his cross.

When I carried the cross, I felt that for those few moments, Jesus on His cross was in my hands.

But not everyone liked the way I carried the cross.

As I was waiting one Sunday, cross in hand, to lead the procession from the church foyer to the altar, the visiting priest who was saying Mass that day said, "Crossbearer, proceed!" His tone wasn't friendly.

I looked at him.

He repeated it, louder this time: "Crossbearer, proceed!"

I said, "My name is Joe."

He glared at me.

He said icily, almost with a sneer: "I know who you are."

And then he said, nearly barking it: *"Crossbearer, proceed!"*

I proceeded to the altar . . . as slowly as possible . . . taking the tiniest baby steps . . . knowing how much I was raising his blood pressure.

On another occasion, a woman in her fifties came up to me in the church vestibule and said, "I've seen your movies, I've pleasure it would give me. I didn't care that she might get pregnant again, that I might cause her to kill her seventh human being, *my own child*.

As much as I was opposed to abortion, that's how much I was in favor of gay marriage. After a long history of endless discrimination against gay people, the Catholic Church was now engaged in the worst discrimination of all. By condemning gay marriage, the church had condemned gay people to a life of promiscuity, one-night stands, and sex as sport. I knew that my own period of promiscuity had ended when I met Naomi. I had always been faithful to her and always would be. I had met the mate who was my other half, who made me complete in every way, even the sexual one. Our marriage stabilized, celebrated, legalized, and solidified our relationship. The church was denying these things to gay people, who were just like Naomi and me except for the fact that they were attracted to the same gender. It was an injustice on every level. By opposing gay marriage, the Catholic Church (that transparently gay organization) was making a mockery of every compassionate, human, and humane thing that Christ stood for.

I felt we needed Jesus at the Temple again—at the Vatican this time, on Saint Peter's Square. We needed Jesus enraged, on a rampage against hypocritical bishops and cardinals formulating church policy . . . Jesus doing another wilding.

I thought it probable those bishops and cardinals were so terrified of coming out of the closet (or being dragged out) that they were willing to engage in the worst kind of homophobia . . . to protect their own pampered, powdered skins.

We needed Jesus again . . . to kick some ass.

———

read your books. Come Judgment Day, *you're* going to be cruci-fied for what you *wrote*."

I looked at her and grinned. There's nothing like coming out of Sunday Mass, sky-high on God, your heart brimming with faith and joy, and getting cold-cocked by some fat biddy who had her head you-know-where.

"What do you do?"

"I'm a nurse," she said.

"On Judgment Day, you'll be crucified for all the patients that you killed."

"I . . . haven't . . . killed . . . any . . . patients," she sputtered.

I smiled brightly.

I said, "We'll see, won't we?"

I knew I had just flunked Christian behavior test number two.

WE BOUGHT Joey a disposable camera when he was six years old. Naomi and I figured he'd waste his shots, but he so badly wanted to take pictures.

On the second day he had it, we were walking out to the car when he said, "Wait a minute!" and stopped. He aimed the camera at the clear blue sky and snapped a picture.

Naomi said, "What are you doing?"

"I'm taking a picture of God," the boy said.

Naomi said, "That's a waste of money, to take a picture of the sky."

The boy looked down at his new camera and, hurt, said, "No, it isn't."

A week later the film had been developed at Kmart, and Naomi took Joey to pick it up. She handed him the packet. It was his first film and she wanted him to see his pictures first. The boy flipped through them slowly. Most of them were blurred. He looked sad.

Then he got to one and stopped. The smile on his face was huge. He said, "You see? I told you I was taking a picture of God!"

Naomi stared at the photograph.

It showed a big, beautiful, clear sky. In the center of the sky was a glorious and ethereal cross emblazoned in white, shining in the sky.

ON CHRISTMAS DAY, Father Dan brought a finger with him to church.

It was a statuette of an index finger, extended on high. Nothing else, just the finger.

He held it up and showed it to us during his homily. He said he had gotten it years ago as a Christmas present, and when he first got it, he didn't understand why anyone would give him a finger as a present.

But as he kept looking at it, he said, he understood. The finger pointed straight up—to the sky, to heaven, to God. It was a constant reminder to always think about God during the course of the day. Father Dan said he now thought the finger was one of the best Christmas presents he'd ever gotten.

Father Dan walked to the back of the altar when he finished his homily and sat in the chair next to Deacon Fred, a handsome, devout man with a powerful, deep bass voice.

Father Dan handed Deacon Fred the statuette of the finger as he sat there and said, "Hold this for me." And Deacon Fred, without batting an eye, instantly said, "It's not the first time you've given me the finger." Both men had their mikes on, so we heard every word of it clearly.

There was a moment's silence, and then the congregation exploded in noise. Some of us laughed. Some of us groaned. Some of us booed. Some of us clapped. Deacon Fred, mortified, looked like he wanted to flagellate himself. Father Dan was tomato red.

Some of us were still grinning when we gave each other the sign of peace.

# PART TWO

# HOPE

*And not only that, but we also rejoice in our afflictions, because we know that affliction produces endurance, endurance produces proven character, and proven character produces hope.*

**—PAUL'S LETTER TO THE ROMANS 5:3–4**

WE SAT in the same place at Holy Angels Church each Sunday—three or four rows from the front, in the center section.

We knew our neighbors by name: Susan, who was Hungarian, usually sat with her daughter and an older lady, Cornelia, whom she'd met in church and who was also Hungarian. Terry, who also carried the cross sometimes, sat with his wife and teenage daughter. Anne and Betty were in their seventies and sat right behind us. Joe was in his seventies, too, and he usually sat with Betty. "We're just friends," Betty said, "for companionship, you know." Kitty, who was in her eighties and gorgeous, sat with her daughter Kathleen, who was in her forties; they both usually had rosaries wrapped around their hands. John, who read the Epistle sometimes, sat with his wife and young daughters; they were a great-looking family. Neil sat nearby sometimes. He was a rolypoly man in his sixties, a nationally known motivational speaker and a church celebrity because his daughter was a network news correspondent.

They were our "church friends," our "church neighbors." We chatted before Mass each Sunday—talking about health and about vacation plans—and discussed at great length and with great seriousness what the Indians or the Browns or the Cavs had done the previous week. We talked a lot about the weather, and sometimes vague dinner invitations were issued in the effusive spirit of the moment but were rarely acted upon.

The truth was that we were a little uncomfortable when we ran into one another outside of church—at Giant Eagle's sausage section, or at Bob Evans or McDonald's or that new taco place next to the Movie Gallery.

We were surprised to see one another, and seeing one another outside the church context was somehow jarring. The warmth and effusiveness of church, the *high* of church, were missing when we met like this—our conversations were short and rushed, as though we were in a hurry to get away from one another here and meet where we usually met and where we were supposed to meet. In church. When we saw one another at the fish fry in the church basement, this awkwardness wasn't there. Even though we weren't in the "worship space" together, we were still okay. It was as though the church walls themselves offered us support.

Since we were church neighbors, there were neighborhood rumors alive here, too. Why hasn't Andy been to Mass with his wife and kids for two straight Sundays? Was there something wrong with the marriage? And why was Cindy looking so pale? She wasn't having a recurrence, was she?

When one of our church neighbors disappeared suddenly and was gone for more than a month, we were bereft. Was it illness? Was it death? Was it a weakening of faith? A decision to no longer worship God each Sunday? We were frightened then, and when we gave one another the sign of peace before Holy Communion, we held our neighbors' hands for an extra moment and squeezed just a little harder.

We were frightened because we knew that we could get sick, too. We could die, too. And was it possible that we, too, could experience a weakening of faith and stop going to church? Stop coming here to see our neighbors on Sundays?

So we prayed and we asked God to give us the strength to believe in Him, to keep us among our church neighbors whom we loved and hardly knew.

———

THE GENTLEMEN of the men's fellowship at Holy Angels Church asked me to join them one evening and tell them how I came to discover the presence of God in my heart.

I told them after some deliberation that I couldn't do that. I was afraid that if I talked about my moment on the way to Damascus, God would think I was bragging and get pissed off at me.

My relationship with Him was a relatively new one, and I didn't want to do anything to screw it up.

I certainly knew that He could get easily miffed. His divine nose snapped out of joint easily. He needed some anger management pretty badly. Check out that tsunami in Indonesia. Check out Hurricane Katrina. Check out the fact that my beloved Cleveland Indians hadn't won a World Series since 1948!

That really scared me. Somehow His nose had gotten out of joint about Cleveland. I didn't want to mess with someone who could stay pissed off at the lowly, woebegone Cleveland Indians for *sixty years*!

So the gentlemen of the men's fellowship at Holy Angels would just have to do without me. Some other reformed sinner could talk about who or what he had in his heart. I was chickenshit.

AFTER I FOUND GOD, I wanted to write something in celebration of my discovery of Him.

I heard that an agent I knew in Hollywood was representing a project called *From Saul to Paul,* the story not unlike what had happened to me.

I called my agent friend and volunteered to write the screenplay for *From Saul to Paul.* I told him about my spiritual rebirth and explained that since I had lived this story myself, I could write this piece from the inside out. I could literally put heart and soul into it.

He laughed at me and said, "From *Showgirls* to God, from *Basic Instinct* to Paul."

I didn't get the job. I couldn't help feeling that my discovery of God had actually worked against me. My Hollywood agent friend didn't want *Saul* to write Saul's story. He wanted someone "more objective, someone with a more secular approach," someone who viewed Saul as a *Star Wars*–like figure, laser cross in hand.

My agent friend told me, though, that he was happy to hear that I, like Saul, had found God. "Me," he said, "I'm sorry to say I haven't found Him yet, but I *am* dating a Ukrainian model who would knock your socks off."

I reciprocated and said I was happy to hear that, too.

SIX MONTHS after my throat surgery, Marshall, my surgeon, thought he saw something suspicious in my throat again. Another growth, he feared.

Another surgery was called for.

The morning of my second surgery, I got up at dawn and felt strangely calm. I didn't even take the Neurontin he had prescribed for anxiety.

I wanted so badly to live, but I had learned that it wasn't up to me. I had learned that nothing was up to me anymore.

*Thy will be done, not mine.*

In the harshly lighted operating room, the Stones were blasting. As much as I loved them, I didn't really hear them, although I knew that He had sent me "Jumpin' Jack Flash" as a sign of His affection for me. This almighty Dude, I was learning, really did have a wild-ass sense of humor!

I didn't hear the Stones because in my head I was singing another song, one that Christie, our choirmaster at Holy Angels, had written: "Lord, I ask You for courage, Lord, I ask You for strength, be with me now, be with me. Lord, I ask You for courage, Lord, I ask You for strength, I put my life in Your Hands."

Marshall was smiling when I opened my eyes. No sign of any cancer. Just some granulated scar tissue from the first surgery.

"GOD IS GOOD," Father Dan kept saying, and looking back at my life, I realized how good God had been to me.

I was born in Hungary at the end of World War II. God took me from the war zone to first a British and then an American refugee camp. God brought me from the refugee camps to America, the greatest, richest country in the world. I grew up piss poor with seemingly limited horizons, and God made me a journalist who was given a gold medal at the White House. I went to work for a magazine in San Francisco and was so poor that Gerri and I had to scrounge through our pockets looking for spare change for food. And then God made me a screenwriter who made millions of dollars. One day God sent me packing with Naomi and our four boys back to Cleveland, where I'd grown up. Cleveland was also home, it turned out, to the most skilled throat surgeon in the world, who diagnosed my throat cancer after it had been misdiagnosed in California and who then saved my life by performing a radical throat surgery that had never before been attempted in America.

Yes, God had been good to me: I had seven children—three grown—all of whom (thanks be to God) were in excellent health. My father lived to be ninety-four years old and died peacefully of old age.

I was married to a woman whom I adored, the woman who was my perfect partner, smart and beautiful, who came from the same ethnic roots that I came from, who was also from Ohio and also a journalism/English major. The best mother that I ever met, Naomi was the sunlight of all our lives.

Yes indeed, God had been good to me; Father Dan was right.

But why had it taken me so long to see that?

Why had it taken sixty years for me to realize God's goodness?

Why had I banished Him from my life all these years—while He was being so good to me?


I WANTED TO THANK GOD for helping me by doing something to help others.

I decided to write an op-ed page essay for *The New York Times*.

I wrote: "Smoking was an integral part of many of my screenplays because I was a militant smoker. I have been an accomplice to the murders of untold numbers of human beings. . . .

"So I say to my colleagues in Hollywood: What we are doing

by showing larger than life movie stars smoking onscreen is glamorizing smoking. What we are doing by glamorizing smoking is unconscionable.

"Hollywood films have long championed civil rights and gay rights and commonly called for an end to racism and intolerance. Hollywood films espouse a belief in goodness and redemption. Yet we are the advertising agency and sales force for an industry that kills nearly ten thousand people daily.

"A cigarette in the hands of a Hollywood star onscreen is a gun aimed at a twelve- or fourteen-year-old. The gun will go off when that kid is an adult.

"We in Hollywood know the gun will go off, yet we hide behind the smokescreen of phrases like 'creative freedom' and 'artistic integrity.' Those lofty words are lies designed, at best, to obscure laziness.

"I know. I have told those lies. The truth is that there are a thousand better and more original ways to reveal a character's personality.

"Screenwriters know, too, that some movie stars are more likely to play a part if they can smoke—because they are so addicted to smoking that they have difficulty stopping even during the shooting of a scene. The screenwriter writing smoking scenes for the smoking star is part of a vicious and deadly circle.

"My hands are bloody; so are Hollywood's. My cancer has caused me to attempt to cleanse mine. I don't wish my fate upon anyone in Hollywood, but I beg that Hollywood stop imposing it upon millions of others."

The media response to my op-ed piece was overwhelming. I did the *Today* show, *The Edge* with Paula Zahn, Deborah Norville's *Inside Edition,* and Fox News. *The Chris Matthews Show* came to Cleveland and did a whole hour on my "anti-smoking crusade."

The Cleveland Clinic's new director of communications, Angela, who'd been educated at the Kennedy School of Government and worked formerly for NBC, convinced me to set up a grassroots antismoking group in association with the Clinic called "Join Joe." T-shirts were ordered; red JOIN JOE—YES YOU CAN wristbands were planned. A Cleveland Clinic Web site, Join Joe/Cleveland Clinic.org, was set up in cyberspace.

The Cleveland Clinic also paid for a series of antismoking public service announcements (PSAs) that were filmed in Los Angeles. Tony, the director, had previously brilliantly directed the film *American History X* with Edward Norton.

I stood and looked into the camera and said this: "I used to think smoking was so cool, so hip, so rock and roll. Then I got throat cancer. Cancer isn't cool, hip, or rock and roll. Cancer hurts. Cancer makes you cry. And then it kills you. Please— don't smoke."

In the other PSA I said: "Hello. My name is Joe Eszterhas. I'm a screenwriter. I always glamorized smoking in my movies. I thought smoking was cool. Then I got throat cancer. Maybe that's my punishment. Please—don't let Hollywood sucker you into smoking. Please—don't let people like me kill you. Don't smoke."

As I did one take of the PSA, there were tears in my eyes. Tony used the take with the tears—it played in hundreds of movie theaters and on television stations across the country.

I felt Join Joe was beginning to make an impact. On the Join Joe Web site, hundreds of people were able to pinpoint the movie and the actor that first influenced them to light up a cigarette.

I flew to Los Angeles and had meetings with studio heads, directors, and producers. I tried to convince them not to use smoking scenes in their films. Many of these people, it turned out, agreed with me. They said the movie stars were at fault.

I wrote an article in *Variety* condemning movie stars for killing people while they publicized their pet charities in front of congressional committees. I did television and radio talk shows blasting them and singling them out by name for their callousness and irresponsibility.

It looked like the campaign was working. Kirk Douglas wrote an article in *The New York Times* urging actors to stop smoking onscreen. Bruce Willis said in an interview that he'd never smoke onscreen again.

*But . . .* exactly at that moment, the Cleveland Clinic went through a change of leadership. The new head of the Clinic hired his own head of communications and Angela was gone, doing PR in New York and Los Angeles. Because Join Joe had been Angela's pet project, Join Joe was dead, too. The Web site was gone, the T-shirts were collector's items. The red wristbands finally arrived by the thousands and were distributed to the different Clinic campuses around Cleveland and Florida.

I never got one. I finally called and a public relations person in the new administration sent me some.

I felt good about what I had done. The best way to thank God for helping you, I knew, was to help others. I told every interviewer I spoke to during the Join Joe campaign that I couldn't have quit smoking without God's help.

I was His witness. Some of the reporters I spoke to wrote down the things I said about God. But none of them mentioned Him in the stories they wrote about me.

———

BACK IN MY DRINKING DAYS in Malibu, I'd get up very early in the morning sometimes to do interviews for the *Today* show. The interviews were aired between seven and eight in the morning East Coast time, which was four and five West Coast time, but I'd get up at two o'clock in the morning to wake myself up.

By "wake myself up," I mean I wanted to be lucid and articulate enough to be speaking to millions of people on television.

To be "lucid and articulate," I drank a bottle of ice-cold white wine between two and four in the morning. Thus fortified, I was ready to pontificate in dazzling thirty-second sound bites.

The first time I did the *Today* show after I stopped drinking, I had to fly to New York and do it live in the studio. I was petrified. I had to speak to millions of people *sober*? After more than forty years of always having had some kind and quantity of alcohol in my system?

Monstrous butterflies fluttered their wings together inside me. I was short of breath. My muscle memory kept reaching for the bottle of gin-filled Evian water that I used to carry around with me on special occasions.

I said a prayer.

I said another prayer.

I said another and another.

The prayers had a much greater effect than the gin and the white wine ever had. Pearls of wisdom and golden butterflies came fluttering out of my mouth. For the first time ever, Katie Couric liked me.

SHORTLY AFTER the Katie Couric interview, a television reporter from Germany came to interview me about smoking in films. She'd hired a crew from Cleveland to shoot the interview. I knew some of the guys in the crew from previous interviews.

I did the interview in the living room of my home, and in the course of it I told the reporter how much God had helped me to stop smoking and drinking.

"What?" she said. "God? You believe in *God? You?*" Her eyes were saucers.

When we were finished with the interview, she asked if we could walk around outside while the crew shot some B-roll without the sound of the two of us talking.

We got outside and I saw that she had noticed the small ceramic statues of Jesus and the Blessed Virgin Mary in our backyard, facing Naomi's kitchen window. The reporter went over and whispered excitedly to the camera crew.

She asked me if I would stand in front of the statues, and I told her that this interview wasn't about God, it was about smoking.

"But you believe now, no? *No?*" she said.

I said yes.

"Then you stand with statues?" she said.

I said no, I wouldn't stand in front of the effing statues.

She went over to the crew and whispered to them again.

She and I started walking around, and I noticed the crew guys craning and distorting themselves at various angles so they could get shots of the statues in the background while we walked.

I said to them, "Hey, guys, what the eff are you doing?"

One of them shrugged and said, "I'm sorry, Joe, but she's red-assed about getting you in the same shot with Jesus."

"Fine," I said, "I'll stand with Jesus."

I stood in front of Jesus's statue. The German reporter was happy.

A month later, on the Internet, Naomi found a photograph of me that had been in a German magazine. It showed me standing next to the statue of Jesus in my backyard. Somebody had drawn a halo above my head.

GOD hadn't just been good to me. He had literally saved my life on so many occasions.

When I was an infant during World War II, a bomb struck the Hungarian apartment house where we were living. It blew me out of my mother's arms and collapsed the building around me. An old lady found me among the ruins and put a babushka over my mouth so I wouldn't choke on the dust and debris.

When I was a little boy in the refugee camps of Austria, I was the only kid there who didn't get tuberculosis; several of my playmates died.

When I was thirteen and running crazy on the West Side of Cleveland, another kid my age pointed a zip gun at me and pulled the trigger. He blew his own hand off.

When I was in college, drunk one night after many beers, I got into my car and raced it down a hillside, skidding on the ice. The car spun around in circles and overturned in a ditch. I walked away unhurt.

When I was in college, hung over on a Sunday morning, I stalled my old clunker of a car on some railroad tracks. I heard the train coming, leaped out, and ran. The train missed my car by inches. It was on another track.

When I was in college, driving home on a two-lane road after too many gin-and-tonics, I was about to pass a car that indicated it was turning right. It turned left instead, and I drove off the road at seventy miles an hour. My car jumped a ditch and slammed head-on into a tree. The car was totaled. I walked away unhurt.

As a young reporter in Cleveland, I went drinking with a colleague. We were heading home when he made a sudden left-hand turn with his VW Beetle. My passenger-seat car door swung open and I fell into the middle of a busy street, cars zipping by in both directions missing me by inches. I got off the pavement in the darkness and staggered away unhurt. My colleague was so out of it that for miles he didn't even notice I was gone.

As a young reporter in Cleveland, I found myself in the middle of a shoot-out between police and black militants. A cop I knew and liked bled to death a few feet in front of me as I huddled behind the tire of a police car and wet my pants. Except for the pants, I was undamaged.

As a young reporter in Cleveland, I interviewed a Hells Angel who had killed three people and was still on the loose. He suddenly freaked in the middle of the interview that I would tell police where he was hiding out. He put a sawed-off shotgun to my throat. His finger was on the trigger and he was shaking badly. His eyes were red, his pupils dilated. I talked him out of pulling the trigger.

When I was in my thirties, I did so much cocaine that I permanently altered the interior of my nose. A girl, a gram of coke, and a bottle of gin was an almost nightly menu. One night I stopped being able to speak from seven o'clock until six the next morning. I was able to formulate my thoughts but unable to articulate them. I kept snorting and drinking and partying, though. Every other part of my body still worked. The next morning, when I was able to speak again, I went to see my doctor. He told me that I had suffered a small stroke, which easily could have killed me. He warned me that I had to stop doing cocaine immediately. I didn't stop for another year—when the same thing happened again.

When I was no longer a young man, I picked up a stripper at a bar and took her back to my hotel. We were both drunk and stoned but seemed to like each other. She pulled a gun on me from her purse when we were both naked and said, "Give me one reason I shouldn't pull the trigger." I talked *her* out of killing me, too.

When I was no longer a young man, an artery burst in my nose (probably from high blood pressure and years of heavy drinking). I had to be rushed to the hospital before I bled to death. I made it . . . barely.

There were at least four near-death airplane experiences, too: a flight where we lost so much altitude over the Atlantic that we could see the waves whitecapping; a flight to Maui where the obviously drunken pilot told us that the flaps weren't working and we had to detour to Honolulu, where the runway was longer; a flight to Chicago where we had to ditch all our fuel before we attempted an emergency landing because the landing gear didn't work; a flight to Dallas where, as we were about to land, the pilot rocketed the plane up again as all the baggage came out of the racks above.

All of that was prelude to my throat cancer, caused by the madman drinking and demented smoking I had done since my childhood.

I realized now that most of these near-death experiences had been caused by my self-destructive, self-abusive, dark, and sinful behavior. Yet for some reason God had chosen to spare the sinner's life on all these occasions.

I had never even stopped to realize that God had to really love me . . . to save my life over and over and over again.

I realized it now, though. I knew that God loved me more than I deserved.

Why had God saved my life? What was His purpose?

Did He save my life so that I could write *Basic Instinct* and *Showgirls*? So that I could raise six children? So that I could proclaim His love and glory to the world? Was it pick one or all of the above?

I had two fundamental questions: Why in the world was I still here? What had I done to deserve God's love?

MY MOTHER'S LIFE, in contrast, was a nightmare. Her mom died at fifty of cancer, and after her death her father advertised in the newspapers for a new wife. He married a whore.

He got syphilis from her. My mother watched her father treat himself for his syphilis with a long needle that he stuck again and again into himself.

My mother suffered a nervous breakdown shortly after her dad remarried, and she went to live with another family for a year. Months after she went back home, she married my father.

Nazis and Communists were invading Hungary, and she gave birth to me in a barn while she and my father were fleeing the country. Bombs were falling everywhere. Nazis and Communists were shooting at one another and at anything that moved. My mother, my father, and I fled.

We spent six years in refugee camps in Austria. We came to America and were hungry and poor. The Americans made fun of our accents and clothes. My mom developed schizophrenia.

She heard voices beamed from outer space. She decided my dad and I were demons. She stopped speaking to us. She chain-smoked. She didn't speak to us, but she blew her cigarette smoke at us a lot. I shied away from her. As the years went by, I walled my heart against her.

She developed uterine cancer. It spread to her lungs. It spread to her brain. It spread everywhere. Hard little purplish red lumps popped out of her skin everywhere.

Even though she wasn't speaking to us, she held my hand when she died. I kissed her hand the moment after her death. My hands were bloody from the way she'd clawed into them in her final hours. She was fifty years old when she died—the same age as her mother at her death. I was twenty-three.

Through all of that, *all of it,* my mother loved God.

She said the rosary every day. She never wavered in her faith. She sat at the kitchen table drinking black coffee and smoking her Herbert Tareytons, praying.

For a very long time I was angry at God for what He did or allowed to be done to my mother. She'd lived an awful, tortured, God-damned life.

What could my mother possibly have done to deserve such a life? How I marveled that my mother never lost her faith.

I knew now what an amazingly strong woman my mother was. Because she had God at her side . . . didn't she?

ED AND NOREEN were our closest church friends. We had randomly sat near them when we started going to Mass at Holy Angels. They were both in their fifties. He was a mild-looking man with an obvious fondness for the Indians jacket he wore so often. She was a strong-looking woman with an appealing twinkle in her eye.

As church friends do, we started chatting about nothing much:

the weather, the Indians, the Browns, the Cavs. Then, as Clevelanders do, we started talking about our ethnic backgrounds—Ed
was Polish, Noreen was Irish, and Naomi and I were a mongrel
mix of Hungarian, Italian, and Polish. "Our own little United
Nations," I called it, and that made Ed and Noreen laugh. We
talked, too, about Ed's antique mint-condition Thunderbird,
which was the center of attention in the church parking lot on
sunstruck spring or Indian summer Sunday mornings.

One day I got a letter from Ed that touched me. My new
church friend had noticed that I wasn't going to Holy Communion while Naomi was. He wrote to tell me to forgive myself for whatever it was that was stopping me from receiving
the Eucharist. Ed wrote that he knew I was a good man de-
serving of the body and blood of Christ. He wrote that I was
denying myself nourishment that would help my recovery and
my life.

I called and thanked him for his letter.

"You're not angry at me, are you?" he asked.

"No. Why would I be angry at you, Ed?"

"Well, it really isn't any of my business. I really had no right
to write you a letter like that."

"It's okay," I said. "I appreciate that you care enough to have
written it."

"I wrote it because I'm your friend," he said.

"I know that," I said. "Thank you."

And so we became—Ed and Noreen and Naomi and I—
more than just church friends. We crossed that rarely crossed
line that limited church friendships to the worship space. We
went for appetizers at their house (Ed, a good cook, took pride
in them). They came to our house for nonalcoholic "cocktails,"
as Ohioans still call them. They brought us a wreath for Christmas that they had made themselves. We took them a poinsettia

plant. We went to all the Lenten fish fry dinners in the church basement together.

Naomi and I liked them a lot. Noreen was funny; she had an impish and direct sense of humor and especially liked needling me: The boys were getting really big, huh? Pretty soon now they'd be bigger than me. "How's that going to feel, big guy?" Noreen said. Or: "I saw you on TV doing an interview. You were pretty good. Isn't that stuff a waste of time, though?" (I agreed that it was.)

Ed asked a lot of questions about the boys, maybe because Ed and Noreen didn't have any children. I said to him: "We should put a sign on our door that says 'Animal House.' Every other day all the food in the fridge has been eaten up. Every other day we're out of toilet paper. The plumber is on a retainer."

They knew about my cancer, and both Ed and Noreen said they were praying for my recovery. They never mentioned that Noreen had cancer, too. They never mentioned that she'd been fighting it for a long time. We found out when I stood up in church during the annual Blessing of the Sick and Noreen, a few feet away from me, stood up, too.

Ed told me the story. She had been fighting it for nearly a decade. It had begun as uterine and then metastasized. She had been through innumerable rounds of chemo and radiation. But the most amazing thing about Noreen, Ed said, was that she never, *ever,* allowed her ordeal to get her down. She worked throughout all of it, hardly ever missing a day at the office. She worked in a real estate office, overseeing properties. Very often she'd have the chemo in the morning, then go straight back to the office and head right out to look at homes. Ed said, "She believes that God will get her through this somehow and that meanwhile she should do the work that God made her good at."

I saw, too, how completely in love Ed was with Noreen. He had dedicated his life to her, through God. He had asked God to save the love of his life, and he was doing everything he could to convince God to do it. He had become a Eucharistic minister. He went to the seven o'clock Mass every day (while Noreen got ready to go to the office). And he became Father Dan's chief assistant. Ed arrived early to open the church and stayed late to close it.

Noreen, as usual, was as *direct* about her cancer as she was about everything else. "I know the cancer isn't going to kill me," she said. "One of these chemos or medications will." I asked her quietly, when we were alone, if she was afraid of dying. Because I too was a cancer survivor, it was a question I had a right to ask. She answered it with heartbreaking directness: "I'm only afraid of what's going to happen to Eddie." At one of those Lenten fish fries, she even jokingly introduced us to one of her friends. "She's going to take care of Eddie," Noreen said, "when I'm gone."

As the years went by, we shared numerous crises with Noreen and Ed relative to Noreen's cancer. Ed began calling us after her chemos and exams to let us know how she was doing. We found ourselves waiting for and dreading the calls. The news was rarely good. Her condition looked hopeless several times, but each time she somehow rallied. It was so grave once that a twenty-four-hour prayer vigil was held for Noreen in our little church.

Naomi and I attended, of course, and we found Ed there, his eyes wet.

"Where's Noreen?" I asked, expecting to hear the worst.

"Where do you think?" Ed said. "At the office."

It was so perfectly Noreen, and I admired it so much. A whole bunch of people were on their knees in church praying for her, tears in their eyes, begging God for mercy, and Noreen was out in the world trying to sell a house.

I realized then that in my fight against my own cancer, Noreen had become my hero, my role model. She'd been fighting her horror for a *decade.* She'd been fighting her horror with balls and grace. She didn't allow her horror to monopolize or dominate her life. She had marginalized its cruelty, objectified its ravages. You can try to kill me, Noreen was saying to her cancer, but I'm not going to let you stop me from doing what I do. *I'm going to sell another house, damn you!*

Sitting next to her in church one day, I reached over and held her hand, which had a rosary wrapped tightly around it. We stayed like that till the end of the Mass, hand in hand, never looking at each other, two cancer survivors staring straight ahead. Holding Noreen's hand, like Holy Communion, gave me strength.

I knew, too, at that moment, what holding Noreen's hand reminded me of. I had once held my mother's hand in church the same way. My mother's hand had also had a rosary wrapped tightly around it. My mother's cancer, too, had begun as uterine before it metastasized. My mother, too, had dealt with her cancer just as directly: She had worked as my father's assistant till her very last days, never allowing her surgeries and treatments to interfere with her work.

Holding Noreen's hand gave me the strength to face all the details of my mother's dying, details that I had forcibly banished from my memory through the years.

*Oh God,* my mother died when she was only fifty years old. And when they did the first exploratory surgery, when she was only forty-five, they thought it was possible that she was pregnant. But it wasn't a baby, it was a massive baby-size tumor.

She had four other major surgeries before it was over. I

walked her around and around in our backyard for hours, holding her by the hand, for exercise, for strength, and she didn't say a word, just stared off blankly, holding her rosary. And when finally it was ending, when she could drink only Coca-Cola syrup and eat a bite of a hot dog, she gasped for air in her bedroom at home surrounded by oxygen tanks, purple black tumors sticking out of her body everywhere, even on her face.

*Oh God,* she held my hand as she died and clawed it bloody. We called the John J. Hriczo Funeral Home when she stopped breathing, and when their hearse got there with its body bag, it couldn't get in our driveway because exactly at that moment the garbagemen were there making their pickup.

*Oh God,* her bedroom reeked of a stink so foul after she died, a stink unique to dying cancer patients. And the roses in the backyard died the day after she did, and *Oh God,* a year to the day after her death that foul, hellish stink came back. For no reason except to remind my father and me how much she had loved us.

*Oh God,* I loved my mother so much.

And I hated God so much after she died, hated Him for most of my life, until the day I sat on a curb in Bainbridge Township and, sobbing, asked Him to help me.

Holding Noreen's hand in church now with its rosary wrapped around it, thinking about my mother with tears in my eyes, made me remember what Ed had written to me in his letter. To forgive myself for whatever it was that was stopping me from receiving Holy Communion.

As I prepared to receive Holy Communion now with Naomi and our boys and Noreen and Ed, I knew I had forgiven myself.

*Oh God, graced by Your love and loving You in return, I have finally forgiven myself for hating You.*

———

MY FATHER, meanwhile, had always low-keyed God to me. He went to Mass on Sundays and sometimes sang in the choir, but he was often at war with something or other that the priest had said from the pulpit.

"Did you hear that *hülye*," he'd say on the way home from church. "That whole thing was *hulyeség*." *Hülye* meant "simpleton," and *hulyeség* meant "simpletonlike behavior."

He'd tell me things like "God helps those who help themselves" and "Don't pray for it, do it!"

I knew part of his problem was that he'd spent too much time around the priests he worked for at his Hungarian Catholic newspaper. "What all of these so-called men need," my father said to me when I was grown, "is a good sexy woman." He winked and said, "Or a good sexy man, I don't care which, it doesn't matter."

But now, after his death, I realized that as much as my father had always low-keyed God to me, he did go to Mass *every Sunday,* mostly by himself after my mother's death, and he did receive Holy Communion *every Sunday.*

When the nurses at the nursing home where he died gave me his personal effects, they gave me his glasses, his watch, his wallet, and a Hungarian prayer book. That was all.

His wallet contained an expired driver's license, a photograph of my mother before she got sick with cancer, and a photograph of me as a ten-year-old fifth grader at Saint Emeric's School, a boy whose face was filled with acne and freckles. It also contained a list of my phone numbers—"in case of emergency."

The prayer book was worn, its pages nearly off the binding

and underlined in many places. The front flap also had a list of my phone numbers—"in case of emergency."

Holding this old prayer book, I knew that my father may have low-keyed God to me, but he had also said a lot of prayers.

I HAD a miserable existence at the Catholic high school I attended.

I was dirt poor. The kids, the brothers, and the priests were middle- and upper-middle-class. They made fun of me. For my accent, my greasy used brown paper lunch bags. For my haircut. For my pants, too worn and too short.

The brothers and priests made fun of me first, and then the kids imitated them to curry favor with them.

Nearly forty years later, I had a photograph of the high school I'd attended in my office at home. My high school had been razed. The photograph was of a great big pile of rubble.

One of the brothers who made fun of me and humiliated me in high school wrote me a letter when I was a wealthy screenwriter living in Malibu.

He was teaching in Arizona at a school for American Indians. The school needed money. He asked me for ten grand.

I wrote him a letter. "Considering how badly you treated me at Cathedral Latin," I wrote, "considering how un-Christian your behavior was, you're not getting a penny from me."

He wrote me a letter back asking me for forgiveness. He said he'd pray for me.

I wrote him back enclosing my contribution: one dollar. I said nothing about forgiving him. I said I'd pray for him, too.

With God in my heart, now, I thought of that brother who'd asked me for ten grand.

I thought of how I'd said I'd pray for him but never had. I wasn't praying back in those days.

But I was praying now, and I decided to include him in my prayers for one week. I wrote him a note saying I'd finally forgiven him. I enclosed another dollar with my note.

I realized when I sent him the dollar that it was possible I'd failed yet again in my attempt to live a good Christian life.

WHILE WE WENT TO CHURCH every Sunday, I told Naomi I didn't want the boys left alone for a split second while we were there.

If any of our guys had to go to the bathroom, one of us always went with them. And since little boys went to the bathroom all the time, Naomi and I went to the bathroom *a lot*.

When the boys had to take religious instruction classes in the church basement before their first Holy Communions, we went with them. We didn't drop them off. We sat there next to them all during the sessions.

And when they went to Reconciliation with Father Dan just before their First Communion, I insisted that the door be left open so we could keep an eye on them . . . and I was told that was the new church policy anyway. The door now always had to be left open.

It was a ridiculous, ironic situation. While I was back in church, praying to my God, I was afraid of what would happen to my boys there in some dark corner, or down in the church basement where the fish fries were held, or in the shadowy, dimly lighted chapel where the Blessed Sacrament was always on display.

I explained to our boys that a priest was a "stranger" just like other strangers. And they had to conduct themselves accord-

ingly. *You don't know them, so stay away from them and don't talk to them even if they talk to you.* Our boys followed the rule. Father Dan spoke to them warmly, and the boys listened politely but said very little and looked away.

I was back in the Catholic Church, but I was also a good father. I made sure that no harm would come to my boys in the church where I spoke to God.

At the same time, Naomi and I decided that we wouldn't give a penny to the church.

In its time of trouble, the church was desperate for money. We heard pleas from the pulpit for cash with what seemed to be increasing emphasis. We knew why. Settlements in mind-boggling multimillions had been reached with those who'd been molested by priests. Now we were being asked to contribute the hush money. Now we were being asked to help bribe those who'd been savaged into keeping the details of their savaging out of the newspapers and television shows.

I asked Father Dan if it was possible to make a donation to the church and be certain that the money wouldn't wind up as part of a sexual molestation settlement.

Father Dan said sure. "Just make your check out to the church building fund."

But I didn't believe him. Not that I didn't believe Father Dan personally; I didn't believe his superiors: He was in the employ of the Catholic Church. And the Catholic Church was lying about every facet of this scandal—minimizing the number of priests involved, denying that the church hierarchy had known very much about it.

Yet every day, damning new evidence emerged proving that criminal priests had been protected and sheltered from charges by their superiors. It became painfully clear that this was a church whose pharisees-in-charge were liars, perverts, and enablers.

Another issue was emerging, too. As the sex scandals got more publicity, cases of "financial misappropriation" by church officials were popping up in headlines. Right now in Cleveland, a former bishop was being accused of keeping secret bank accounts, one of them filled with nearly a million dollars. Two other highly placed diocesan lay executives were being accused of stealing millions from church funds.

Who knew, then, where the money that went into the church collection basket was winding up? In a pedophile defense fund? In the retirement benefits of an ousted priest-perp? Or in the back pocket of a big-shot church mogul who wanted to refurbish his secret getaway condo?

Yes, I was a Catholic again, but this was a different church from the church of my childhood; this was a haven for child abusers, liars, and thieves.

Maybe not, though. Maybe the church had *always* been this way. I suddenly thought of my old and good friend Father John, the priest who'd helped me so much when I was a boy. But Father John had secretly had a wife and the two daughters he'd raised in another town. Where, I suddenly wondered, had my priest friend gotten the money to afford doing that on his measly priest's salary?

That collection basket, I knew firsthand, had always been *such* an inviting target. I remembered seeing all those baskets filled with little envelopes stuffed with cash in the sacristy of Saint Emeric's Church when I was an altar boy. *All those little envelopes filled with all that cash!* I had barely resisted their temptation, stopped only by my fear of stealing God's own money. But I knew other altar boys who hadn't resisted those fat little envelopes, who dined on cheeseburgers at the Royal Castle (financed by the collection baskets) for weeks.

This was *some* homecoming! I was crossbearer in a church

where we were paranoid about leaving our boys alone for even a few moments in the church building itself. And where we couldn't contribute any money to God's cause because we were afraid it would wind up in the hands of pedophiles, liars, enablers, or corrupt and hungry altar boys.

Not long after Naomi and I started going to church, we were in Las Vegas for a film festival, and on Sunday morning we found a Mass near the Strip.

The priest looked like a Vegas priest: He wore a badly fitting toupee and what looked like a painted-on (too thickly) tan. He was in his sixties.

He began his homily by welcoming the tourists and wished us all "good luck at the tables." And then he said: "Every time you pick up a newspaper, you read something about another awful thing that a priest somewhere has supposedly done. Lies. More media lies. Media lies designed to hurt Christ."

Then he said, "One bad apple doesn't spoil the whole barrel."

One bad apple? *One?* When there were *thousands* in this particularly putrid barrel?

I remembered what Father Bob had said in our kitchen after he'd said the First Communion Mass for our sons Joe and Nick. I was telling him how outraged I was by this pedophilia scandal and its cover-up, and one of our guests interrupted to say, "Oh, no, I don't think this is that widespread." And Father Bob had said to him, "Unfortunately, you're wrong. This is just the tip of the iceberg."

And I remembered what Father Dan had said after the articles started appearing in the newspapers: "The other day I was walking in downtown Cleveland. I was dressed as a priest. I have always been tremendously proud of being a priest. It has always made me feel special to be recognized as a man of God.

But that day I found myself zipping up my jacket to cover up my collar. I was walking with my head down, afraid. Afraid that someone would approach me with condemnation. I felt sad. I felt so sad."

The priest in Vegas went on blaming the media, but Naomi and I didn't want to hear any more of it. We got up and started to walk out of the church. There was a sudden silence from the priest as our footsteps echoed through the church on the long walk out.

And then we heard the priest say, "Good-bye." And then we heard him say, "And good riddance."

He got no laughs from the congregation. They sat there in silence. Naomi and I were encouraged by that.

Our first Sunday back at Holy Angels, Father Dan quoted the writer-priest Andrew Greeley in his homily. Father Greeley said, "If you think you've found the perfect church, join it. But understand that when you join it, it will no longer be perfect."


FATHER BOB ASKED ME FOR a favor. He was involved in a project to do a series on priests for the local PBS station.

He asked if he could bring the outline over to my house for suggestions.

We read through it together. The outline was fine, but I saw the title for the series at the last moment.

"You've got to change this immediately," I told him.

He was startled. "But why?"

"You're not looking at the title in all its implications," I said. "Especially considering all the stories about priests in the media right now."

Father Bob thought about it a moment, turned red, and said, "Oh, my God, thank you."

The title was *Beneath the Cloth*.

A NONDENOMINATIONAL MEGACHURCH had opened its doors just down the road from us. Its pastor was earning a national reputation for his spirituality and eloquence. He had even appeared in a Hollywood film starring Jim Caviezel from *The Passion of the Christ*. Some media types joked that Jesus was the pastor's costar.

One Sunday morning, our patience with Catholic Church scandals waning, Naomi and I took the boys down to the megachurch. We were not only angry about the pedophilia and the church's cover-up, we were also tired of one too many Holy Angels homilies that had put us to sleep. Father Bob's homilies had always kept us awake: He even used props (a ladder in front of the altar once) to startle us to attention. He became a clerical drill sergeant when necessary to hold our attention. "Are you *awake* this morning? Is it *that* difficult to clap your hands?" Father Dan could never be accused of acting like a drill sergeant, clerical or otherwise. Weighed down by the brutality of his weekly parish schedule, he sometimes seemed a little sleepy. And Deacon Fred, who was allowed to sermonize on relatively infrequent occasions (thank you, God), drove us all bats by repeating most sentences twice (in a six-minute homily) and constantly referring to someone named "Cheeze-us."

The megachurch was everything I thought it would be. The congregation was upscale and white-collar suburban. Folks were decked out in their Sunday best; there were no Rolling Stones T-shirts here, no T-shirts at all. Most people wore suits and ties and dresses. They addressed one another (and us) as "Brother" and "Sister." Kids were carted off to a Sunday school room far removed from the worship space. (I had to insist that our boys were staying in the worship space with us; it was obvious that the usher with the freeze-dried smile who told us about "the children's center" wasn't happy.)

Our worship space itself was like a large college lecture hall. There were visual aids, even . . . a videoscreen at the front of the room flashed words to the songs that were being sung. Everyone in the room had a well-worn Bible in hand and underlined sequences as the preacher spoke. The chairs we were sitting in weren't pews; they were soft padded chairs like the ones I'd sat on so often in fancy Hollywood screening rooms.

The pastor, who wasn't giving the sermon today, was a thin, good-looking man with classic looks. I saw immediately how much a movie camera would take to him. Not that there was anything over the top or theatrical about him. He was low-key, and he spoke with a quiet humility about his faith in God. He quickly introduced the man who would give that day's sermon, a fiftyish visiting Bible scholar and professor from Indiana.

The professor began his sermon by describing the joy of growing up in a little Indiana town, the same town he would attend as a college student. He said he used to ride his bike around the meadows in the town each day and revel in its beauty. He spoke of the many places he had lived and how he loved that little Indiana town more than any of them. He spoke of his love for his wife and children.

He then read a psalm that described the joy and importance of raising a child. How you could shape a child at an early age to grow up to be something glorious. He said that in our society today, women were out in the marketplace in full force. Being a "homemaker" had somehow become less important. That as a society we claimed to have furthered the value of women because they now climbed corporate ladders and attained executive positions previously held by men. And in doing so, they were paying others to raise their children.

"There is no greater responsibility," he said, "no greater challenge, no more rewarding career, than to raise a child! It is shaping our future! What greater fulfillment can there be than guiding those who will take our place on the world's stage? How can anything, any job, be more important than raising a child? Than instilling in a child goodness and joy and optimism and the will to achieve? Why put this enormous responsibility, this great gift, into the hands of someone else?"

He ended by thanking his parents. He named them and talked about the little house in Indiana where they still lived and where he grew up. He described a childhood so enriched by his parents that, thanks to them, he grew up to love and treasure life itself. He traveled the world and accomplished many things, and then he passed his valued lessons on to his own children and, through teaching, to others.

When he was finished, he was choked up, as were many of us. His tears weren't for effect—he loved his parents so much that talking about them made him cry. He had moved us, but he had done it by making us think, a combination rarely in evidence during a Catholic homily. Our hearts were soaring as we walked out (even the boys had paid attention).

Now that is the kind of homily we need to hear every Sunday, I thought.

But something odd took place in the next few hours after we got home. Yes, that sermon had been great, but . . . as moving as the sermon had been, that's how empty the service itself had felt. I talked to Naomi about it and she felt the same way, and we finally understood what we were feeling:

*We missed our little church.*

As we thought and talked about it, we realized it was the Mass that we missed. The Mass was our guiding prayer, not psalms from the Bible. Holy Communion was our prayer's climax, and there had been no Communion at the megachurch. We missed hosting the body and blood of Christ in our hearts and bodies. We missed it so much that we started making phone calls to see if any parish had a Mass that afternoon. (None did.)

We had talked so much about the lack of powerful, moving homilies in the Catholic Church, and here we had experienced as powerful and moving a sermon as it was possible to experience . . . and we suddenly didn't care about it. We cared about trying to find a Mass. The powerful sermon ultimately didn't matter. We needed Communion, the body and blood of Christ, like two starved vampires needing to feed on Christ's grace.

It may have been a church full of pedophiles and criminals covering up other criminals' sins . . . it may have been a church riddled with hypocrisy, deceit, and corruption . . . but our megachurch experience taught us that we were captive Catholics.

I DIDN'T GIVE UP. I badly wanted to mesh my newfound faith with what I did for a living, so I kept my eyes peeled for a suitable movie project.

I saw a piece in *Variety* about a producer who had the rights to a story that I thought would be ideal for my talents.

It was about a young woman named Ashley Smith and a black man named Brian Nichols. Nichols was being held in the Atlanta jail when he escaped. He killed a judge and two sheriff's deputies during his escape and held Ashley Smith hostage for a long night in her suburban apartment. A former drug addict whose husband had been killed in a shooting, she read to Nichols from the Bible and from Rick Warren's bestselling book *The Purpose Driven Life* and talked to him about how God helped her beat her addictions and regain control of her life. Empowered by her faith, Ashley Smith talked Nichols into letting her go and giving himself up to the authorities.

I thought I saw a riveting thriller here, a scary, harrowing hostage drama that would pull audiences in with its tension levels and send them out with a message about God. It was the message I wanted to put out there as a way of thanking God for what He had done for me. I thought the story would fit me perfectly: The guy who'd written thrillers like *Jagged Edge, Music Box,* and *Basic Instinct* would now write a faith-based, God-loving thriller with *Jagged Edge* elements.

I asked my manager to track down the producer I'd read about who had the rights to the story. His name was Lou. He was in his seventies and had made a career out of producing faith-based "Christian" films. He'd produced a film starring Dean Jones as Charles Colson, the Nixon aide who went to jail, found God, and started a worldwide prison ministry. He was also producing a project, soon to be released, directed by Michael Apted, an esteemed British director, and financed by Walden Media, a Christian entertainment company that had bankrolled *The Chronicles of Narnia.*

My manager reported back that Lou was at first in utter disbelief that the man who'd written *Basic Instinct* was interested in Ashley Smith's story, but then said he was "thrilled" and asked that I call him.

I called him. He was certainly unlike any other producer I'd spoken to in my thirty years of writing screenplays. His conversation was full of "blessings" and "God bless you" and "Thanks be to God." The names he dropped weren't those of industry people (except for Walt Disney, who'd paid for Lou's education), they were Christian political figures: George Herbert Walker Bush and George W. Bush and, mostly, Chuck Colson, who was a friend of Lou's. He told me a story about how, once in Washington, he had seen Colson and Eldridge Cleaver, the Black Panther who had found God, hugging. Then, almost as an afterthought, after minutes of "blessings," he told me he didn't want to do the Ashley Smith story as a film. He had a deal with Lifetime Television and they already had a writer who'd do it as a TV movie. Sorry, Lou said, and signed off with "God bless you" and more "blessings." He even said he'd pray for me, and in return, observing the Christian protocol, I said I'd pray for him, too.

But I didn't. I was pissed off and maybe a little hurt. I wasn't used to being turned down for a project, especially one that I passionately wanted to do. And, of course, I thought Lou was an imbecile to do this film for a small cable television company when the story could have been a powerful, perhaps even award-winning, film with two great parts and huge worldwide box office potential.

One day about six months later the phone rang, and it was Lou. After a lengthy barrage of "blessings" and attestations that he'd been praying all this time for my health, he told me that his Lifetime deal had fallen apart and God had told him, he said, to call me and see if I was still interested in the project—which Lou was now willing to do as a feature.

I was interested, but I told him there was a specific way I wanted to tackle this story. I wanted to do it absolutely factually, with no embellishments. I didn't want to do the usual Hollywood version of a true story—a true story either "based upon" or "inspired" by real events. I wanted to do it with the veracity of a documentary. I wanted to interview both Ashley Smith and Brian Nichols myself at great length and write the script from their accounts. There wouldn't be a line of dialogue in the piece that didn't really take place. If their two accounts varied in places, then I wanted to use both accounts, from the different points of view, in *Rashomon*-like fashion.

Lou didn't say anything for a while, and then he said, "What are we going to do about this drug business?"

I knew that Ashley Smith had beaten drugs with God's help the same way I'd beaten both booze and cigarettes. That was part of the story that made it so appealing to me—in a sense, I'd be writing about *my* struggle through *her* struggle.

But this wasn't, I realized, what Lou was talking about. Lou explained that his Lifetime deal had collapsed because the media had discovered that Ashley Smith didn't just read from the Bible and *The Purpose Driven Life* that night. She had also given Brian Nichols drugs—drugs that she said she wasn't using but still possessed in the new apartment she had just moved into. It also turned out, the media discovered, that she'd had several opportunities to get away from Nichols that night—he'd even let her get into her own car as he'd followed her in his—but hadn't. And now there were rumors, false, vicious, ugly rumors, Lou said, all over Atlanta that she had done more with Nichols that night than just give him drugs.

I told Lou that none of those things concerned me. I would find out what was true from my own interviews. As far as I was concerned, the more human the story turned out to be, the more powerful it would be. We were all weak and we were all sinners. Lou said he couldn't argue with that and sent me the transcripts of the interviews Ashley had done with the ghostwriter of her book, and I began poring over the material.

I finished about a week later and told Lou that while I believed

Ashley's story and thought she was courageous and heroic, I thought it was essential that I be allowed to interview Brian Nichols before I wrote a word of the script. He said he would get to work on trying to arrange that right away with Nichols's lawyers.

He called me two or three times a week to see how I was doing, to "check in." In this regard he was like every other producer I'd ever worked with, who had always called when they had nothing to say except, "I'm just checking in." The difference was that while a producer like Robert Evans "checked in" with obscenities and scatological humor, Lou checked in with "God bless you" and the endless and continuing "blessings."

Lou kept talking about God. He said it was a "God-incidence" that I had found him just shortly after he had gotten the rights to this story. God had arranged this, he said. God had been the agent who'd hooked me up with Lou and with Ashley Smith's story. At one point he even said that God had saved my life just so I could write this story. (If that were true, I thought, it would make God more ruthless than Michael Ovitz: You give a man throat cancer just so you could get him to write a script for you? In my one-on-one battle with Ovitz, then Hollywood's most powerful figure, he had threatened to destroy my career but not to give me throat cancer.)

One morning Lou called to tell me he was on the way to the annual House of Representatives prayer breakfast, then called *from* the prayer breakfast to tell me that he had drawn Chuck Colson aside moments ago and told him, "We've got Joe Eszterhas—he's on *our* side now."

And Colson had said, "Thanks be to God. That's a great win for our side."

Lou said he even mentioned to Colson that maybe, just maybe, Lou could talk me into writing a remake of the Chuck

Colson story since the original had turned out to be such a gigantic stiff.

*Chuck Colson?* I thought. The same Chuck Colson who'd helped Richard Nixon in his quest to turn this country into a tyrannical banana republic? And now I was on *his side? And Richard Nixon's side?*

I'd never be on Chuck Colson's "side." Eldridge Cleaver may have hugged him, but Cleaver in his final years was such a ding-a-ling that he spent much of his time designing a pair of pants that had a codlike device that would make your thingamajig look bigger.

Lou and I kept talking about Ashley's story, and he asked me one day if I had any thoughts about who could direct the script well. I mentioned Tony, who had directed *American History X* with a gritty, powerful, documentarylike flair and who had directed my antismoking videos.

"I don't know him," Lou said, and paused as though to pick his words carefully. "Is he Jewish?"

Well, that was picking your words pretty carefully all right.

I said, *"What did you say?"*

Lou said, "Well, you know, I'm not saying anything, of course, but this is such a Christian story, it just might be better if we had a Christian director for it."

*Is he Jewish?* The age-old question asked through the years by so many, too many, too *tragically* many Christians.

"I don't see this as a Christian story," I said to Lou. "It's a human story and ultimately a faith-affirming story, a pro-God story, but not a Christian story."

"Well, yes," Lou said, "it is all those things you mention."

I left a message on Lou's machine a few days later and told him that I was sorry, but I had decided to do another project instead, although there was no other project. I ended my message with "God bless" and enough "blessings" to gag even that great man of God, Chuck Colson.

I WAS STILL TRYING to live a good Christian life. Lian, our Guatemalan housekeeper, got a call one day from her two younger sisters. Maria and Blanca, both in their late twenties, were at a police station in Woodmere, a suburb near us. They were about to go to jail, they said.

I knew Maria and Blanca. They had filled in for Lian sometimes and had watched the house and dogs when we were gone on vacation.

So I got in the car with Lian and drove to the Woodmere Police Department to see if I could help. I saw Maria and Blanca sitting in a holding room, petrified, pale. They were so happy to see me that Blanca lunged and tried to kiss my hand.

I talked to one of the young cops who was handling the case. He was a nice guy. He knew they were illegal aliens, but he said he wasn't interested in "that aspect of the case."

This was the case: Maria and Blanca had been caught shoplifting at a nearby Target. They had stolen jewelry—two fake gold bracelets—and cosmetics. A videocamera had caught them; the stolen items had been found on "their persons."

I took the young cop aside into a corridor by the pop machines. "I've known Maria and Blanca for years," I said, "they've worked for me. They've been in my house when I've been gone. Nothing has ever been missing. Nothing." It was true.

"If you charge them with this," I said to the young cop, "they're going to have to come to court and their illegal status might become an issue—do you want that to happen? Over some cheap bracelets and lipstick?"

He said, "There have been some other thefts at other Targets around the area. They match the description we got from the other stores."

"What was taken?" I asked.

"The same kind of stuff," he said. "Bracelets, lipstick, other cosmetics. Junk."

"I'll pay for all of it," I said. "Whatever was stolen from any other store."

"You must really like these people," the young cop said.

I said, "I came to this country as a refugee too a long time ago. I'm just trying to make it a little better for them. I'm just trying to be a good Christian, that's all."

He nodded and looked at me like he understood.

"Are you a Christian?" I asked.

"I'm Jewish," he said.

We grinned at each other.

I said, "Well, you're a good Jew, aren't you?"

"I try to be," he said.

I said, "There you go."

He shook his head and laughed a little. "Okay," he said, "get 'em out of here before I change my mind. But tell 'em if they get caught again, they're gonna be in a lot of trouble."

They hugged me and kissed my hands when we left the police station. They were so happy, they were crying. I told Lian to tell them in Spanish that if they got caught again, they'd go to jail for sure. Both Maria and Blanca swore that this was the first time they had ever done something like this. They swore on the Sacred Heart of Jesus that this was the first time. And they swore on the Sacred Heart of Jesus that it would never happen again.

I said, okay, the Sacred Heart of Jesus was good enough for me.

They were so grateful for what I had done that the next time we went on vacation, Maria and Blanca came to house-sit for free.

It was about a month later that we noticed that our passports were gone. I had always kept our passports in a wooden box on top of a dresser near our bathroom. The passports had been in there for years. I had seen them there just before we left on vacation. Now they were gone.

I knew Lian hadn't taken them. She'd been with us too long and had had too many opportunities to steal from us. But Maria and Blanca had been in the house alone, and as far as I knew, no one else had been there. Our passports, an immigration official told me when I reported them missing, were worth as much as twenty thousand dollars on the black market.

I didn't want to ask Maria and Blanca if they had stolen our passports. I had no proof that they'd taken them. But I finally decided that I had to ask them. They were the only suspects.

I called and asked them, and they were mortified. They started to cry. They swore on the Sacred Heart of Jesus that they hadn't taken them—*the Sacred Heart of Jesus!* That was good enough for me. I believed them. I was trying so hard to be a good Christian.

OUR NEW BISHOP came to Holy Angels. He was visiting many parishes, introducing himself to his new city.

He came from Boston, a diocese that had been nearly bankrupted by the priest sex scandals. We heard that our new bishop had been shuffled from his old diocese, allegedly guilty of overlooking too many accusations, too many claims.

Our new bishop seemed to me to be a man of stylistic

gravitas—tall, good-looking, articulate, blessed with a booming baritone, a man who seemed to not find displeasing the mellifluous tones of his own voice.

But I knew a little about gravitas, too. Someone who watched me carry the cross one day said, "There he is, Mr. Gravitas!" *The New York Times* once wrote that my face was like a clenched fist.

So at Holy Communion I stepped into our new bishop's line, and as he handed me the body of Christ, I glared at him with my clenched fist of a face.

I knew I'd gotten his attention because as I stood in line afterward to shake his hand, I felt him watching me closely as I approached.

He smiled, but before he had a chance to say anything, I said, "May God bless you, Father, and *forgive* you and give you strength in these troubled and *shameful* times."

My prayer wiped the smile off his face.

Our new bishop said nothing. He seemed to be trying to catch his breath. It was as though I'd slapped him. I shook his hand. I kept going. I glanced back and saw him watching me.

Our new bishop looked frightened. That was good. I liked that. I suddenly had an overpowering urge to scare the piss out of all the bishops in all the dioceses in the world.

For the good of the Catholic Church. For the good of all of us.

I HAD A BORN-AGAIN FRIEND who had dedicated his life to Christ. He prayed much of the time.

He had a gambling addiction, so he prayed that the Indians beat the Yankees, that the Browns beat the spread, that LeBron score more than thirty points.

He prayed nonstop on Friday nights because his son was a star of the Kenston Bombers high school football team, and he always bet on his son.

At first I was judgmental about my friend. About all the praying he was doing to win his bet. Petty and self-serving, I thought, a waste of God's time.

God was dealing with wars and tsunamis and genocide and cancer and AIDS, and my idiot friend . . . who loved God . . . was asking Him to bless LeBron tonight just so he could make some money off Him.

I couldn't believe the silliness of that the more I thought about it. God wasn't his copilot; God was his bookie.

But then I decided that I had no right to judge my friend. It was possible that beating the spread was as important to him as beating smoking and drinking was to me.

If that was the case, of course, it meant that my friend was an idiot and so was I for thinking that the spread and smoking and drinking amounted to the same thing.

But even idiots needed God's help, I decided. Even idiots could love and believe in Him and ask Him for His help. I figured out that maybe God had a special affection for idiots because idiots generally behaved idiotically and therefore got the short end of the cosmic stick.

Maybe what was most important wasn't the nature of the request that we addressed to Him, but the fact that we got down on our knees and asked Him . . . *anything*—even the stupid spread against the stupid Steelers.

Did that mean that tsunamis and cancer and touchdowns and genocide and missed free throws all had the same importance within the cosmic scheme of things?

I didn't know, but I wasn't going to bet on it either way.

———

EVERY MONTH or so I got an offer to write a script. It was always the same script they wanted me to write, and it was usually for the same enormous amount of money.

I kept refusing the offers, even though my bank account was shrinking, much of my money gone to a whopping divorce settlement, the upbringing of four ravenous boys, and staggering medical and hospital expenses.

"God will provide" was a phrase I kept hearing in my head. Repeating it to myself made it easier to turn down the offers.

The reason I turned down all the offers was not that I didn't want to write screenplays anymore. I loved writing scripts—I'd written more than forty of them during my thirty years as a screenwriter. (Sixteen had been made into films.)

The reason I turned down the offers was that I didn't want to write dark stories filled with sex and violence.

I explained this to a producer one day on the phone, and he said, "Where the hell's your head at, then?"

I told him: My head was in loving my wife and playing with and raising my boys. And it was in taking long walks in the sun, the rain, and the snow. And it was in seeing how the Cleveland Indians were doing. And it was in that turtle I rescued from the road yesterday by picking him up by the tail and turning him loose in our lake. And it was in trying to develop my relationship with God.

"You're turning a million dollars down because you picked a turtle up by its tail?" he said.

"I guess so," I laughed.

I finally did take a screenwriting job. It was an offer to write a script about the Hungarian revolution of 1956 against occupying Soviet forces—a piece of history right out of my roots.

The script had violence in it, but then it was about a violent (and heroic) revolution against forces of tyranny, oppression, and godlessness. It had a little low-key intimacy in it, too, but certainly not the bombastic baba-boom big-bazoom campy sex that there was in *Showgirls,* for example. I wrote the script for peanuts as a labor of love.

I knew what everyone wanted from me. I hadn't become "America's king of sex and violence" (*Time* magazine) or "king of the icepicks" (*Time* again) accidentally. Everybody in Hollywood wanted me to write the *Basic Instinct/Jagged Edge* kind of thriller where you were terrified and wet at the same time. I could write that kind of script half-sober (I wrote several that way), but I didn't want to do it now. I wasn't half-sober anymore, either—I was completely, 100 percent sober and lucid.

But I was trapped. I knew I'd have to make some money quickly.

I was scared. I prayed and kept saying, "God will provide, God will provide, God will provide," to myself.

I prayed. And I prayed. And I prayed. And I prayed.

And one day, I got an envelope in the mail. It was a plain brown envelope and I almost put it aside thinking it was another bill. But I opened it and inside was a check for a lot of money, a whole lot of money.

The sequel to *Basic Instinct* had begun shooting in Europe. I'd had absolutely nothing to do with the sequel, but I was entitled to this money by my contract for the first *Basic Instinct*. My contract said even if I wrote not a word of the sequel, I still would be paid.

I'd been saved by a miracle. By my prayers. And by a movie

I'd had nothing to do with that was filled with sex and violence (that I didn't write).

God had provided. With a miracle. With a wink and a nod, too.

FATHER DAN kept talking about "God-incidences" in life. There was no such thing as a coincidence, according to his theory. There were only God-incidences, times when God chose to interfere directly in human life.

On our trip to Hungary to research the film I would write about the Hungarian revolution, *Children of Glory*, I experienced "God-incidence" myself.

I hadn't been to Hungary since I was taken from the country as an infant by my parents. While there on this research trip, I wanted to visit the grave of my paternal grandfather, József Kreisz, whom I'd never met. He'd been a teamster in Hungary, a Russian prisoner of war who'd spent years in Siberian prisons, a tough, no-nonsense man who adored his family and settled disputes with the world mostly with his fists.

I knew how much my father had loved his father and how much he had missed him in his life. They'd been separated by World War II: My dad came to America, and my grandfather stayed in Hungary. My dad had often spoken to me about visiting his father's grave before my dad died, but as it turned out he hadn't been able to make the trip.

I wanted to make it for him.

I wanted to go to my grandfather's grave for my father.

I went to the cemetery in Kispest shortly after we arrived in Hungary. It was the working-class Budapest suburb where my father had grown up and where my grandfather had lived all of his life. I asked the cemetery officials how to find József Kreisz's grave, but they told me their records were incomplete and scattered. They weren't computerized, and Kispest had several cemeteries. All of them had been ravaged by bombings during World War II.

In addition, all of the Kispest cemeteries were being "reconstructed" now. It meant, I discovered, that some graves would simply be wiped out while others would be moved.

They asked me what my grandfather's address in Kispest had been. I didn't know. They told me that without his address or date of death, they'd be unable to locate his grave. I didn't know his date of death, either; I'd been a very little boy when he died, but that's all I knew. The cemetery officials said they were sorry, but it was impossible. They couldn't help me.

I was sad. I'd even planned to leave my father's driver's license on my grandfather's grave as a kind of symbolic gesture, a way for my father to visit and say good-bye, through me, to his father.

I tried frantically to reach Budapest census officials to find József Kreisz's address, but I was told that all of their records had been destroyed by bombs, too. There was no one else I could ask—I knew of no other relatives either in America or in Hungary.

I didn't know what to do next, but I asked God to help me. I didn't want to go back to America without having knelt at my grandfather's grave.

I had a dream that night. I dreamed that I was a little boy and that my father was writing a letter at our kitchen table in Cleveland to my grandfather in Hungary. My dad put the letter into a blue airmail envelope, and *in the dream I saw my grandfather's address on the envelope:* Ady Endre Utca 70, Kispest.

I woke up and wrote down his address on hotel stationery. In the morning I called the people at the cemetery and told them the address I had seen in the dream.

That afternoon I put a bouquet of roses on my grandfather's grave. Then I put my father's driver's license atop the roses. I knelt there and prayed for a while and thanked God for helping me miraculously to find my grandfather's grave.

I went back to the cemetery office and thanked the woman who had found the grave for me after I had given her my grandfather's address.

I had come just in time, the woman told me, my grandfather's grave was being "reconstructed."

"When?" I asked.

"Tomorrow," she said.

MY AGENTS were telling me to write a TV show. They had been getting calls, they said, from both network and cable television executives "asking about me . . . begging me" to write "an adult, sexy, edgy series."

One of the TV executives, my agents said, had declared that "Joe Eszterhas's head is where sweeps ratings lie."

A cable exec had even called with a specific idea: Would I be interested in writing a series called *Crimes of Passion,* a series "where sex and violence intersect"?

One of my agents said, "Nobody does it better. That's where you live and breathe."

But I wasn't living and breathing there; I had moved away deep into the Heartland, into a red state where I carried the cross many Sundays. How could I explain to my Hollywood agents that I was gone, that I was living and breathing a new relationship with God, which I treasured—and which, besides my family, was the most important thing in my life?

I had thrown away the ice pick (*Basic Instinct*), the knives (*Jagged Edge* and *Sliver*), and the Dogon hatchet (*Jade*). I kept a Bible nearby. I wanted to write about my new faith . . . and about God and His relationship with man. But I knew my agents wouldn't have understood any of that, so I didn't say anything.

I said, Yes, writing a TV show was an interesting idea. I said, Yes, maybe one of these days I'd come up with an idea and send it to them.

And one day a few months later I did come up with an idea for a TV show and I sent it to them.

It was called *Saviors*.

My agents . . . they just . . . well, they nearly *befouled themselves* in disbelief. *This* was my idea? Did I actually expect them to sell . . . *this*?

*Saviors*?

Naturally they said what agents have always said in such situations: My outline was *brilliant,* yes. It was *revolutionary,* sure. It was *groundbreaking,* you betcha. It was *incendiary,* even.

But they would never . . . *ever* . . . be able to sell it. They used the word that was the kiss of death in Hollywood: *noncommercial*. My brilliant, revolutionary, groundbreaking, incendiary idea for a TV show was also unsellable.

I knew what that meant, thank you very much. Blessings and more blessings, see ya later (much, much later), Elvis had left the building. It was time for me to get the eff out of the auditorium.

So I said fine and went on with my red-state life, my TV show as dead as the Indians' chances to win the American League Central.

A month later, one of my agents called me back. He had been out to lunch with Mark, a successful television producer who was one of the producers of the hit show *24,* the hottest show on television. Mark had asked about me over lunch, and my agent had told him about *Saviors,* and Mark had said he wanted to see the outline that very afternoon. So my agent had e-mailed it to him, and Mark *loved* it. Not just *loved* it, but *really really really* loved it. Mark had *flipped out.* Mark had lost his mind over it. Mark wanted to call me right away. Mark was sitting by the phone waiting to call me.

I said, Okay, Mark could call me.

Two days later, Mark called me.

He said he wanted me to come out to L.A. to talk about my outline. He said the outline was brilliant, revolutionary, ground-breaking, and incendiary. And he thought it was commercial. By "commercial," he meant he thought People Out There would watch the show, but Mark said he thought it would be "very difficult" to get the show past "the Gatekeepers," the television executives in charge.

The executives, Mark said, "got very, very nervous at any mention of God." Mark said, "God has never been big in prime time. God, camouflaged in secular wear, has been on marginal cable television, but never network or prime cable prime time." Mark said he would happily fly to Cleveland so I wouldn't have to fly out to L.A., but "I've just got too many projects that I'm juggling right now."

Naomi and I flew out to L.A. to meet him. He was in his forties, lanky, dark-haired, a well-groomed man who spoke very fast—it must have been all those juggled projects weighing on him, I thought.

Mark wanted to know the genesis of my idea, and I told him about sitting there on the curb that afternoon and sobbing, asking God to help me. Mark stared at me for long seconds, his mouth almost agape, and said, "Wow!"

Then he said it again: *"Wow!"*

I asked him if he believed in God, and he smiled thinly and glanced away from me and said, "Sure, most of the time, absolutely." Then he switched subjects and talked about "the Gatekeepers" again, the television executives "we're going to have to play dodge 'em with on this."

In order to effect our dodge 'em—"I know these A-holes," Mark said—he made some suggestions to "mainstream" this outline, "to commercialize it further." Mark said he was talking only about the outline, not the show itself. Once the Gatekeepers had bought the outline and green-lighted the show, Mark said, I could do whatever I wanted with the show itself.

"You're going to be the show runner," Mark said. "Joe Eszterhas. Everybody knows you don't eff with Joe Eszterhas"— and here Mark gave me a big wolfish smile—"even if Joe Eszterhas has been saved."

I went home and expanded my outline for *Saviors,* "mainstreaming" it, "commercializing" it. I said a prayer after I finished. I said: "Dear God, I think this show is a good idea and I'd love to write it, but if You think these idiot Gatekeepers are going to eff this whole thing up, then please don't let it happen. *Your will be done, not mine.*"

The focus of the show was a fictional priest named Jack Turek. He was thirty-six years old, the pastor of Our Lord and Savior Church. He grew up in a working-class part of Cleveland, the oldest of five siblings; his dad was a retired steelworker. He got into juvenile trouble as a kid, almost went to jail. He got into gangs, drugs, and bikes—even joined a biker gang—then went to war and served heroically in Desert Storm. But what he saw or did there changed him . . . and when he came back he joined the seminary, to the great shock of his family and friends.

Jack Turek was an explosive, charismatic priest with a deep, all-consuming belief in God who had forsaken the violence of his past—though we still saw remnants of it sometimes in his manner and his language. He was also a kind, deeply compassionate man with a sense of great goodness about him. There was something inheld and cool about him—the young and the very old were drawn to him, and he had an ease around the streets and around black people that was evident when we saw him at a church on Cleveland's East Side (the city's most decimated poverty area), the sister parish to Our Lord and Savior, Saint Martin de Porres, where Jack Turek also spent some of his days.

He wore his hair longish and, when he was not in church, dressed mostly in Harley-Davidson T-shirts and black jeans and motorcycle boots. He had a tattoo of Christ crucified on his right arm. He drove an old Dodge Duster "beater" and a vintage Indian motorcycle. He played a mean blues guitar, often by himself.

While he believed in Christ as his savior with every ounce of his being, there was nothing namby-pamby about Jack Turek; he was head-on and confrontational and viewed himself as a soldier fighting God's war against dishonesty, poverty, injustice, abuse, hypocrisy, marginalization, and bullying of all kinds. He was even head-on and confrontational sometimes in his prayers to the God he had devoted his life to.

He confronted and battled not only those forces that harmed or threatened his parishioners, but also the monsignors and bishops of the diocese who, Jack Turek believed, had become politician-clergymen and had betrayed the teachings of Christ.

Though he ran a successful parish (Our Lord and Savior had almost five hundred parishioners), his fear-no-man and fight-for-what-you-believe-in style had made him a lot of enemies in the diocese.

Many there were suspicious of him because they viewed him as a mystic who spent hours prostrate in front of the cross, who fasted for a whole week sometimes, who disappeared on his bike for days at a time . . . who sometimes attended American Indian sweat-lodge cleansing ceremonies.

Mark loved my new outline. He conferred at length with my agents, and they developed a strategy. My agents would notify the production companies on a Monday morning that they would be receiving an outline for a new television show written by Joe Eszterhas, whose movies had grossed over a billion dollars, and produced by Mark, one of the hottest producers working in television. The following companies would be notified: NBC, ABC, CBS, Fox, Home Box Office, Showtime, TNT, Lifetime. The production entities would be told that they had until the end of business that Friday to give us an answer. Whoever stood up first for *Saviors* would, of course, get it . . . if "the numbers" (the money) were right. A whole team of agents and managers would hype the production companies to get their interest salivating: my agents, Mark's agents, our managers, and the heads of the television departments in my agency and Mark's.

"Are you going to give any clues to these companies about what they're getting?" I asked one of my agents.

"What are you—nuts?" he answered.

"Don't you think they're going to think they'll be getting something along the lines of *Basic Instinct* or *Jagged Edge* and then they'll read *Saviors* and suffer seizures?"

"We *want* to surprise them," my agent said.

"Into having seizures?"

"Lookit," he said. He had a fondness for the term *lookit*. "Lookit, what do you want us to do? Tell 'em this piece is about believing in God? They'll use your outline for toilet paper if we tell 'em that."

Mark and all the agents and managers wanted me to be in L.A. that week in case any of the Gatekeepers wanted to have a quick meeting or the agents suddenly needed me in the room for a negotiation.

The next day, Naomi and I flew out to L.A. again. We spent a couple of hours at L.A.'s magnificent new cathedral, one of my favorite new places, as soon as we got there. I called Mark and asked if he wanted to have dinner. An assistant said he'd call me right back, but he didn't.

By Tuesday night, everyone but ABC and NBC had "passed." My agents said all the Gatekeepers had said nice things—the word *brilliant* was used a lot—but the project just wasn't "commercial enough" for them. Again I called Mark, who still hadn't called me back about having lunch or dinner, to see what his thoughts were about how things were going. Mark didn't call me back.

By Thursday afternoon, ABC had passed, too. My agents said the head of ABC programming wanted to have lunch with me "as soon as possible" to discuss projects they had thought of and that I might be interested in writing. Mark's assistant called to say that Mark was very busy but would call me on Friday.

Friday afternoon, my agents called to say that there was an internal disagreement among the Gatekeepers at NBC, and NBC wanted to have a meeting with me and Mark immediately. On our way to the meeting, Naomi got a call on her cell phone from my agents saying that NBC had resolved its disagreement. The meeting was canceled. NBC had passed.

*Saviors* was dead and buried. Naomi and I decided to console ourselves by going down to Anaheim to see the Stones in concert. Near the climax of the show, Mick Jagger came strutting and dancing down the long stage, and as he passed us, he looked right at me. He was grinning like some sort of demon, a Gorgon, a loon. He looked a hundred years old. His eyes bored into mine. I looked the devil right in the eye and grinned right back at him.

The next morning, before we left, I called Mark. I just wanted to say thanks for trying and I was sorry we couldn't get together. His assistant said he was at a meeting—on Saturday?—but I could have his voice mail. I left my message of thanks on his voice mail and asked him to call me back.

Mark didn't call me back. I never heard from Mark again.

But Father Jack Turek, the priest I'd created, lived on in my head. I felt him around me.

I considered his thoughts and feelings daily. I had a bookmark that said, "WWJD." It didn't stand for "What Would Jesus Do?" It stood for "What Would Jack Do?"

The Catholic Church sorely needed men like Father Jack Turek—both in the parishes and in the hierarchy—if it was going to survive.

The man who had written *Showgirls* was offering the church its new savior.

IN 1992, in Bainbridge Township, Ohio, a lifelong local resident named Bud was very angry. Everywhere he went, people were talking about the movie *Basic Instinct*. A quick flash of actress Sharon Stone's privates had become one of the most famous scenes in film history, a must-see for the whole world.

A deeply religious man, Bud was enraged that his America had sunk so low. He blamed in particular the writer of the movie . . . *me*. He was incensed when he saw me all over the television channels publicizing my film.

He did some research and discovered that I had written another film, not yet made, about a president of the United States who has a brief fling with a cow. *A cow. A farm animal.*

When he heard about that script, Bud wasn't just angry or enraged anymore. He was apoplectic. Bud and some of his friends set up an Ohio film company that would make godly, faith-based films.

"Anti–Joe Eszterhas films," Bud told everyone.

But the company faltered and then failed owing to lack of scripts and money, and in 1995, now forty-three years old, Bud watched in great pain as I showed up all over the television channels again. I was publicizing my most recent film, *Showgirls*, rated NC-17. Bud heard me say on the *Today* show that teenagers should bring their fake IDs to see the film.

Something crystallized in Bud's head when he heard me say that: *Joe Eszterhas symbolized everything that was wrong with America.*

In the winter of 2002, when he was fifty years old, Bud was sitting with one of his Recreation League assistant coaches at his home in Bainbridge. They were looking at a list of new players eligible to play baseball in the Rec League. He stopped suddenly and stared at a name on the list: *Joe Eszterhas.*

Bud turned to his assistant coach and said, "What is this? Somebody's idea of a bad joke?"

The assistant didn't know what Coach Bud was talking about. The list he was looking at came from the school district where a seven-year-old boy named Joe Eszterhas had enrolled in the second grade. Bud stared at his assistant and said, "Oh . . . my . . . God!"

Nine months after moving my family from Malibu to Bainbridge Township, Ohio, I was sitting in the bleachers, watching my son Joe at a basketball tryout. A man sitting a few feet away from me kept glancing at me and then looking away. He looked exhausted and depressed.

I looked at him, smiled, and said, "Hey, it can't be that bad!" but he couldn't hear me.

I moved closer to him. "Sorry," I whispered as loudly as I could, "I had surgery for throat cancer. Are you all right?"

He barely looked at me. He said nothing.

I said, "You don't look so good. You want a Coke or something? I'll get it for you."

He shook his head and smiled. He wouldn't look at me.

"It's my divorce," he said suddenly. "I think it's going to kill me."

I said, "Yeah, I know, I've been through one. It very nearly *did* kill me. It's okay now, though. Ask God to help you."

He looked at me then, his eyes slits. "What did you say?"

I said, "Ask God to help you."

He said, "Did you ask God to help *you*?"

"I ask God to help me every hour of every day."

He held my eye and said, "I'm doing that."

"Good. Keep doing it. Sooner or later He'll help you."

He nodded and kept looking at me, and then he broke into a smile. "I'm Bud Daniels," he said.

I smiled and said, "I'm Joe Eszterhas."

He said, "Yeah, I know who you are."

A few months later, Bud picked my son Joe to be on his baseball team. Bud and I saw each other often at games. He had a son, Buddy, who was Joe's age, and the two boys liked each

Bud said this wasn't like baseball. "These parents have all paid a lot of money," he said. "They want to win. That's part of what they paid for. But you're *right*. You're right. This should be fun. I'm sorry. And I thank God I have you around to tell me when I'm being an A-hole."

"Hey," I said, "I'm a real expert on A-hole behavior."

"Because of Hollywood?" Bud smiled.

"Because of *me*."

They kept losing. Joe, not a complainer or whiner, started complaining that he wasn't getting enough play time, that Bud's son, Buddy, was getting *all* the playing time. I kept an eye on it the next game and realized Joe was right. I mentioned it to Bud.

I said, "You promised me when I signed up that the kids would get equal playing time."

Bud said, "You're right. It won't happen again."

After another losing game, he handed me an envelope. It was the manuscript that I'd inspired him to write. I read it that night. It was a twenty-four-page treatment for a movie. It was about the presence of God in men's lives and a modern-day Jesus. I didn't like it, but as I thought about it, I decided that I didn't want to tell him that. Bud had said, "I felt the power of the Holy Spirit all the way through as I wrote this."

I didn't want to tell him the truth because I liked Bud and didn't want to hurt his feelings. And there was the other reason: He was Joe's coach and controlled how much playing time Joe got.

Before the next game, Bud asked, "What do you think?"

And I said, "About what?"

And when he said, "My manuscript, what do you think?" I dodged and said I hadn't had a chance to read it yet, I was involved in writing something myself and wanted to finish that first before I read anything.

"I see," Bud said. He looked hurt.

I noticed at the game that while Joe was getting the same amount of playing *time* as Buddy, Joe wasn't getting the ball *at all*. While Buddy was getting the ball *all the time* and shooting and missing. They lost again.

When Joe said this was unfair, I said to him, "Complain. Tell Coach Bud how you feel. I can't fight your battles for you."

Joe said, "I did. I have. He says Buddy gets the ball because the point guard is left-handed and the plays flow that way. But the plays are plays that Coach Bud designed—they're designed to get the ball to Buddy."

"Well, that's not fair," I said.

The team kept losing. Joe didn't get the ball. He was dispirited. Since his teammates hardly ever passed him the ball—and passed it to Buddy all the time—Joe was playing clumsily, too. He looked like a deer in headlights when he got the ball. The kid who'd been a star in Rec League last year had disappeared.

Coach Bud had *disappeared* him.

Now it was my turn to ask Coach Bud to lunch at Mom's Diner. We began with a prayer again. I ordered a salad—I wasn't hungry. Bud ordered his onion rings, his fries, his burger, his milk shake. He lost his appetite pretty quickly, though.

I said, "What you're doing is unfair and not very Christian. You're playing favorites with your own kid, and in the process you're demoralizing my kid and the other kids on the team because they keep losing. The only kid not getting demoralized is Buddy, because he keeps getting and shooting the ball and, incidentally, missing most of the shots. The lesson they're learning, the lesson you're teaching them, is that nepotism works. If you're the coach's kid, you've got it made."

He looked like he was in pain. He stopped eating. The last

thing he wanted to do, he said, was to hurt Joe. He loved Joe. Joe was a great kid. Joe was so good defensively, with rebounds, he said, that he didn't want to use him much for offense . . . so he could concentrate on defense.

I said that was crap, a lie to justify all those shots that Buddy took that didn't go in.

Bud put his head down for a long moment like he was praying. His eyes looked wet.

"I'm sorry," he said quietly. "It's this divorce. Buddy plays us off against each other. It's hard for me to say no to him about anything, and he *wants the darn ball!*"

I felt my pulse quicken.

"You're telling me that *my* kid walks around the house depressed and in tears because you can't say no to *your* kid? Because of your divorce?"

"If I tell him no about something, then he says he wants to live with my ex. If she tells him no, then he says he wants to live with me. I love Buddy. I want him with me as much as I can. He's the most important thing in my life. He's God's greatest blessing to me."

I said, "I didn't pay you nearly a thousand dollars to break my kid's heart. You and your Christianity. You tell me you've dedicated your life to Jesus Christ. Oh yeah? What would Jesus do? Not this! He wouldn't be breaking a boy's heart just to ass-kiss his own son."

"I'm sorry," Bud said, "please, forgive me."

A few days later, at a practice, Buddy broke his hand. It had to be put in a cast. And for the rest of the year, Joe got the plays and the shots that he wanted, missing most of them. Buddy stood on the sideline in a hooded sweatshirt. The team kept losing.

The season ended with yet one more loss. The kids were happy that it was finally over. So were the parents. So was Bud. I was *overjoyed*! We all sort of fled from each other after the last game.

Six months later, I bumped into Bud while I was picking Joe up after a school dance. He was coming out with Buddy, and when he saw me he turned almost completely around—his back to me—so it would appear that he hadn't seen me.

This Christian life, I thought, got awfully secular sometimes.

But sometimes the secular life got very Christian, too.

About a year after Joe's season with Coach Bud, Joe told me about something that had happened during a team sleepover at Bud's house.

I had given Joe a twenty-dollar bill in case the team went out to McDonald's or Dairy Island. And on the way out of Bud's house, Joe couldn't find the twenty I'd given him. Bud told Joe not to worry about it because he was buying burgers for everybody.

But when they all got back to the house, Joe was panicked that he'd lost the money.

"My dad's going to kill me," Joe told Bud.

So Bud helped Joe look for the money. They looked in Bud's house—in the den, the kitchen, the living room, the basement. They found nothing.

Joe was near tears.

"My dad's not going to trust me with any kind of responsibility," Joe told Bud.

Bud suggested they look in his car. It was dark by now, and Joe looked in the front seat and Bud in the back.

Bud suddenly said, "Here it is!"

Bud grinned and handed the twenty-dollar bill to Joe. Bud said, "I'm glad we found it. I wouldn't want your dad to have to kill you." Joe smiled and looked happy and thanked him for helping him.

"But the thing is," Joe said to me now, a year later, "that was *his* twenty-dollar bill, not mine. I saw him from the front seat flick that money from his hand onto the floor. Coach Bud just didn't want me to get in trouble with you, so he gave me his own money."

I stood there, frozen. I knew Bud didn't have a lot of money, certainly not enough money to hand out twenty-dollar bills to boys who'd foolishly lost them.

I turned on Joe. "Why in the *hell* didn't you tell me this earlier?"

"'Cause I was afraid you'd go ape if I told you I lost the money, just like you're getting ready to go ape now."

Joe wasn't a stupid kid, that was for sure.

"So why tell me now?"

"Well, I know you're having some issues with Coach Bud, but I mean—I think he's a pretty good guy sometimes, don't you?"

I kicked the living shit out of Joe then and sent him to bed. No, I didn't. I gave my boy a hug and thanked him for telling me now and told him he was an irresponsible idiot for losing the twenty bucks. Then I sent him to bed. With a little smack on the arm that didn't hurt. He grinned and went to his room.

The next time I saw Bud was at another basketball tournament. He was eating a doughnut at the concession stand. I marched right up to him and I thought he was going to choke as I got closer and closer to him.

Then I said, "Okay. I forgive you. And I'm sorry, too. I can be a real horse's ass sometimes—but I believe you know that already."

I tried to tell him I owed him twenty dollars and handed it

to him, but he just laughed and wouldn't take it. I knew he wouldn't.

"How's Joe doing?" Bud said.

"Great. He just made his school basketball team."

"That's great." Bud smiled.

I said, "How's Buddy doing?"

"He made his school team, too."

"That's great." I smiled.

We looked at each other and grinned.

"Hey," I said, "you wanna go have a burger at Mom's Diner sometime?"

"Will you tell me the truth about my manuscript if we have lunch?"

"Hell, no."

"How come?"

" 'Cause we're friends again," I said, "that's how come."

"Yup"—Bud smiled—"I guess we are."

I KNEW that if I was going to live a good Christian life, I'd have to learn, as Jesus said, "to turn the other cheek." But I didn't know how I was going to do that. I'd always been an "eye for an eye, tooth for a tooth" kind of guy.

When I was thirteen years old, a seventeen-year-old playground bully kept calling me names and/or beating me bloody. One day while he was standing behind the plate at a batting cage, I sneaked up behind him and swung at the back of his head with a baseball bat. He almost died; I almost went to jail. Flash forward to my forties and fifties in Hollywood, where I became renowned for fighting back fiercely when someone tried to mess with my career or one of my precious scripts. I caused one director's heart attack, sent several passive-aggressive producers scrambling for their shrinks, and began the end of one super-powerful agent's career.

Now, as I contemplated the meaning of my newfound Christianity, my "baby faith," I realized that there was an even more problematic underlying issue. I was a deeply cynical man. I had always been a deeply cynical man. Naomi turned often to me and said, "God, that is so cynical!" For example, I believed that the JFK and MLK and Bobby Kennedy murders were all conspiracies. I believed that Lyndon Johnson had been involved in JFK's murder, that Marilyn Monroe had been killed because she knew too much about the Kennedys, that the American government knew that Pearl Harbor was being planned and did nothing to stop it, that Richard Nixon made Gerry Ford his vice president because Ford had promised to pardon him, that Bill and Hillary knew about each other's affairs. I believed that O.J. and the Ramseys did it, and so did Mark McGwire and Roger Clemens. I believed that the presidency was stolen from Al Gore, and I believed that Dick Cheney was the real president of the United States.

As I kept hearing Naomi say "God, that is so cynical!" I kept trying to tell her that there were deep and fundamental reasons for the depth and scope of my cynicism.

As a little boy in the refugee camps after World War II, I watched American GIs buy sexual favors from married Hungarian mothers with chocolate bars and packs of cigarettes. I watched the mothers make that long, hesitant walk, their eyes down, from the barracks to their assignations. I watched their husbands turn away, tears in their eyes, as their wives walked out the door. I watched old ladies in black babushkas turn angrily away as they passed the young mothers on the dirt path. I saw one old woman spit in a young mother's face as she passed her. I sometimes sneaked to watch the coupling itself on a dirty mattress laid on the floor behind the army Jeeps in the barracks that served as the car pool. (I once saw three soldiers take turns with the same mother.) And then I watched the mother walk back into the barracks with her cigarette pack (or packs depending on the GIs' satisfaction, generosity, or number). In one instance, I saw the woman's husband beat his wife to the barracks floor when she presented him with three packs of cigarettes, enough to feed themselves and their children for two weeks with black-market food.

If the refugee camps were a training grounds for cynicism, then the back alleys where I grew up on the west side of Cleveland provided Advanced Cynicism on a graduate level. It didn't take me long to become a participant in the group activities: burgling grocery stores, carrying a zip gun and a knife, stealing cars for joyrides, breaking all the store windows on both sides of Lorain Avenue between West Twenty-eighth and Fulton, rolling sad-eyed drunks, too wasted even to defend themselves as we kicked them in the groin and the head before taking and splitting their few dollars.

Talk about cynicism: I had another "job" at the same time. I was an altar boy specializing in weddings and funerals. I was handsomely tipped at both events by the mourners or celebrants. And how had I managed to get this particular "job," which all of the other altar boys also badly wanted? I had stumbled on our parish priest one summer night as he was having sex with the funeral director's wife in the backseat of his car. He had seen me seeing him with the woman. He gave me the well-paying altar boy gig as a bribe to keep my big fat adolescent mouth shut. I wasn't stupid, and I knew enough about cynicism by then to take the money and say nothing except thank you.

My first job in the real, adult world was perfect for a cynical young man. I was a police reporter on a daily newspaper, covering crimes that had just happened. I wrote about husbands killing their wives, wives killing their husbands, kids killing their parents, dead strangers killing dead strangers. I had a reputation for always getting the story . . . and more. If the paper needed a photograph of a dead child to put on the front page, I could go into the house, interview the mother, and get her to give me that dusty, framed photo on the mantel, sometimes even with its frame. I was such a sympathetic and seemingly compassionate young man! Those mothers just melted *in my arms*—because sometimes I held them to calm them in their moments of grief. I was so good at this kind of thing that I even got a photograph of a dead robber (killed by police) at the morgue. I somehow convinced the young pathologist not only to let our photographer get a picture of the dead guy, but I convinced him to glue the dead guy's eyelids back so he looked alive (and more presentable for the front page).

Those early jobs were all preparation for Hollywood—where there were those who said I became so successful because of how well I knew to play the game. Hollywood was, after all, the coldest, most unloving, cynical place in the world. If I was able to talk Mom into giving me the dead dearest's photo off the mantel, then I could obviously talk any studio head into anything (even giving me three million dollars for a screenplay). Hollywood, my critics said, was my perfect dark playground, my back alley, my batting cage, my refugee camp, my wedding/funeral altar.

But . . . I had given all of that up now. *Now*—after my throat cancer . . . *now*—after my surgery . . . *now*—after the day I cried on that curb . . . *now*—after my plea to God to help me.

I felt the presence of God in my heart now. I felt like a new and newly born man now.

The drug- and booze-filled chaos of my soul had been replaced by harmony. I was trying hard to banish the hobgoblins of the past from my soul: that grinning GI, stark naked, tossing three packs of Lucky Strikes to that naked, humiliated mother . . . that wino in the alley, trembling, trying to shield his eyes from my shoes . . . that good and God-loving priest, not looking at me as he told me I could be the altar boy at all the weddings and funerals from then on . . . that kid at the batting cage, blood gushing from his nose and mouth . . . that dead guy at the morgue, glued eyes staring right into my soul.

My newly found faith was dictating to me now that I had to become a different kind of man than the cold and cynical one I used to be. I had been converted, I knew, in the truest biblical sense of the word, from one life to another, from darkness to light, from coldness, cynicism, and inner chaos to a life of love, compassion, and consideration.

But . . . I really didn't know if I could do it . . . if I could be a truly good Christian.

My son Joe came home from school one day and said a kid in his class just kept messing with him and today the kid had punched Joe in the face and made his nose bleed.

"So what did you do?" I said.

"I don't know," Joe said, averting his eyes from mine. "Not a whole lot."

In other words, my son had turned the other cheek and walked away.

I stared at him, horrified, realizing that what he'd done was what Jesus had said he should do. Joe had done what I had never been able to do in my whole un-Christian life.

"Geez, Joe," I finally said. "Geez."

Joe said, "What, Dada?"

I couldn't say it.

"Well, what?" Joe said.

"Well," I finally said, "you can't do that, you just can't! You can't let him get away with hitting you. He'll just keep hitting you all the time. You gotta at least throw a jab to his face to get his attention."

"A *jab?*" Joe said. "I don't know anything about throwing a jab."

So, thinking about my uncynical new life, thinking about Jesus's teaching, I sat down in the kitchen with Joe . . . and *we prayed together.*

Well, no, we didn't.

We didn't pray together, we probably should have, but . . .

*I taught Joe how to fight.* How to counter and cross, and bob his head, and feint, and jab, jab, jab.

And at the end of our lesson, I said, "You can only hit back. You hear me? The other kid has to hit you first. Only then can you hit him, you got it?"

Joe nodded, gave me a hug, and went joyfully shadow-boxing and jabbing all through the house.

In my prayers that night as I fell asleep, I asked Jesus to forgive me for not telling Joe to turn the other cheek. I pleaded with Jesus that I could have done a lot worse with Joe. I could have told him to coldcock that kid—to swing at him, on sight, and knock the kid cold before the kid knew what hit him. I told Jesus that I could have told Joe to kick the kid in the nuts. I could have told him to jab an extended finger into the kid's eyes. And I pleaded with Jesus that, even in our fighting lesson, I told Joe to focus on the jab, a light punch that didn't do serious damage. I didn't quite try to convince Jesus that using the jab was almost like turning the other cheek, but still.

No dummy, I also told Jesus that I didn't deserve His love. I didn't deserve His forgiveness for acting cynically and coldly much of my life. I assured Jesus that I was trying to live a good Christian life—and I was! But I had a lot of baggage; a lot of

*darkest recesses*

ugly hobgoblins were still lurking around in the ▓▓▓▓▓▓
of my scarred heart.

I was a baby Christian still, I admitted, but maybe the day would come when I'd tell my sons to turn the other cheek (and let their saved, doomed, sinful, converted old man do the ass whooping for them when necessary).

"Turn the other cheek" contradicted everything that I had learned in refugee camps and back alleys, in the city rooms of newspapers and the conference rooms of Hollywood moguls, but: *I was trying, Lord. I was trying.*

I looked sometimes at our littlest boy, Lukey, and I thought, *That's who I'm striving to be like.* Lukey. Who always looked at me with the most overwhelming affection in his eyes (the exact slate-blue color of my father's) . . . eyes full of total, complete, unconditional love.

I thought it not completely impossible (or just barely possible) that the day would come when I could rid myself of my cynicism and look at people with that kind of love . . . Lukey's love, Jesus's love.

But . . . I was still convinced that Dick Cheney was the president of the United States.

DEACON FRED DID IT AGAIN, this time in the chapel while talking to a group of parishioners—this time it wasn't even really his fault.

Deacon Fred was saying that he had a bad back and his doctor told him he'd have to have it taken care of soon. Deacon Fred said he wasn't anxious to do it because surgery on that part of the lower back was tricky.

A woman asked, "What exactly is wrong with your back? Are you sure you need to have surgery?"

Deacon Fred said the surgery was necessary because he had two ruptured discs and asked that they pray for him.

The next day, in church, during the prayers of intention, the woman asked the congregation to pray for Deacon Fred.

"Deacon Fred has to have surgery," she told the congregation, "for his two ruptured dicks."

I went up to Deacon Fred after Mass and shook his hand and said, "I'm praying for both of your dicks to be healed," but Deacon Fred didn't crack a smile.

He said "Thank you." Very evenly.

# PART THREE

# CHARITY

*I said yeah, oh yeah, oh yeah*
*You'll never make a saint of me.*

—MICK JAGGER, KEITH RICHARDS,

"SAINT OF ME"

I REALIZED that God's presence in my heart had made my family, not my career, the prime focus of my life.

Sure, I was still having the usual creative differences with directors, producers, and book editors. I still wrote a zinging, full-torpedoes ahead, burn-all-the-bridges letter or memo occasionally, and I still put my gut and heart and brain into everything I wrote.

But if I lost one of these fights now—and writers always lose more than they win—I recovered quickly. Back in the day, when I lost one of my "creative" fights (which I always managed to turn into a war), it meant a weeklong tequila, bourbon, or beer marathon.

Now I went for a long walk instead. Or played ball or foosball or Ping-Pong or air hockey or Parcheesi or something with my boys.

Or Naomi and I focused and dealt with *their problems* and, our heads and hearts together, tried to make familial Solomonlike judgments about varying "issues" the boys were dealing with.

Lukey, who was six years old, had been invited by one of his classmates to a birthday party. But the party was being held at a bowling alley, and it would also be the site of the celebrating boy's dad's own birthday party (same day, same time). Lukey really wanted to go to his friend's party, but there would be adults there we didn't know, plus the complete strangers who would also be using the bowling alley. So our verdict was no.

No, Lukey, sorry, you can't go. Lukey was disappointed. Lukey was angry. Lukey cried. Lukey wailed. Lukey got sent up to his room for an hour, where he screamed even more. We stood by our decision, pleased that we had made a Solomon-like judgment.

John Law, who was nine, had a problem with a kid on the school bus. The kid kept harassing John Law and harassing him, and John Law, who very much danced to the tune of his own drummer (and who'd been named after John L. Sullivan, the fighter), finally turned around one day and socked the kid in the nose. The kid bled. And cried. And went to tell the bus driver. Who went to the principal, who called us and called the kid's parents.

There was a meeting in the principal's office with all the combatants (and their parents). Where, oh, where were all my world-famous, top-tier Hollywood and literary agents now? Where were Ed Victor and Guy McElwaine and Arnold Rifkin and Jim Wiatt of William Morris and Jeff Berg of ICM at this moment of crisis, when I could really use their advice?

The kid who'd gotten punched by John Law denied that he'd harassed him. We parents gave one another stink-eyes. The principal *rolled* her eyes. A decision was made to install video-cameras on their school bus. The principal herself would review the tapes each day to see if anyone was being harassed or socked. We parents walked our combatants from the ring of the principal's office, our arms around them. Freestyle stink-eyes flew everywhere.

Joe, who was thirteen and no longer tolerant of being called Joey, wanted to participate in a school essay contest about saying no to drugs. He asked me for advice on what to write about. I told him he had to figure it out for himself, but he should write about something that was close to his heart.

"So you do that with what you write?" Joe asked.

"Sure."

"Did you do that with *Basic Instinct*?" He hadn't seen it, but he knew about it from some of his thirteen-year-old friends who claimed to have seen it.

"Well, no, that one—no."

"With *Showgirls*?" He hadn't seen that one, either, but he'd heard a lot about it from friends his age who claimed to have seen it (and probably did) on VH1.

"Um, no, not that one, either."

Joe gave me a look, shrugged, and sulked away. A couple of days later, he said he was finished with his essay and asked me to read it. It was about something close to his heart all right. It was about how his father had said no to his nicotine and alcohol addictions with God's help. It was about how his father had said he couldn't have done it without God's grace.

It made me cry. I gave Joe a big hug and told him how much his essay meant to me. I told him I was proud of him. One day he came home and told us he'd won his school's essay contest. He read his essay in front of hundreds of classmates and parents in the school's auditorium. A local TV station even sent a reporter. Joe Eszterhas was the man of the hour! I realized as I watched my son that the moment meant much more to me than if I had ever won an Oscar.

Nick, who was eleven, got into a full-scale battle with his music teacher. She had given each kid a partner and told them to pick a musical entertainer they wanted to do a report about. The report was to include a song that they would play in class. Nick's partner picked a rapper named T.I., and Nick, who didn't know anything about T.I., agreed. When Nick was working on his report, Naomi helped him with his Internet research. She found that T.I. was a gangsta, that he had been in jail, that every single one of the lyrics to his songs was X-rated: "I wanna wind you and grind you up on the floor" was one of his milder lines.

Naomi was apoplectic. "Nick is eleven years old," she said, "and of all the singers and musicians in the world, this jerk is who he has to give a report about?" I agreed with her. We called Nick's music teacher. "How could you let eleven-year-old kids do a report on a lowlife like this?" we said. The music teacher said she didn't know who T.I. was, didn't know he was a gangsta, but said, "If we start examining the personal lives of people like Mozart and Beethoven, I'm not sure how well they'd stack up, either."

Now Naomi and I were both apoplectic. Mozart in the same sentence with T.I.? Beethoven on the same classroom stage— Beethoven and T.I. together? It was too late to change the subject of Nick's report, so we told him he could give his report but we wouldn't allow him to play a T.I. song in class.

And that's when everything went goofy! Because Nick's music teacher then decided to give Nick, who had previously gotten all A's, a C on his report. Because part of his assignment had been to play a song in class and Nick hadn't done that.

So here we were: Because Nick hadn't played T.I.'s filth in a classroom filled with other eleven-year-olds . . . he'd gotten a C instead of an A.

The teacher was *punishing* him for not polluting the minds of the other eleven-year-olds in her classroom.

We called the principal. We set up a meeting with the principal and the music teacher. Jim Wiatt and Jeff Berg and Guy McElwaine all flew in on the red-eye. *(I wish!)*

So there I sat at the meeting, the man who had written *Showgirls* and *Basic Instinct,* the man who had suggested that teenagers bring their fake IDs to get in to see *Showgirls* . . . sitting in a classroom in Bainbridge Township, Ohio, telling an obviously frightened middle-aged fifth-grade music teacher that *she* was polluting the minds of eleven-year-olds by exposing them to

T.I. and his Eszterhasian lyrics: "We're going to eff like minks, raise rugrats, and live happily ever after," Michael Douglas tells Sharon Stone in *Basic Instinct*.

I pointed out to this fifth-grade teacher, with the principal sitting there, that this was a public school in semirural Ohio, financed by taxpayer money. And if some newspaper or television station was alerted to this situation . . . and just happened to do a story about T.I. being played with a teacher's approval in a classroom . . . the excrement would fly high and smelly.

We all agreed then that no one wanted to see that story on TV or in the newspapers.

From then on, the principal said, the music teacher would have to be familiar with those artists that the kids wanted to do reports about.

The man who had written *Showgirls,* the first mainstream NC-17 movie, had banished T.I. and other gangsta rappers from the classroom of Bainbridge Township.

I was proud of myself. It felt better than any fight I had fought against any director, producer, book editor, or super-agent.

Or—maybe this: Considering how abused and forlorn that fifth-grade music teacher looked after our meeting: You could take the boy out of Hollywood all right, but could you ever really take Hollywood out of this particular boy?

MUDDY, our eleven-year-old bulldog, was killed by a FedEx truck in our driveway while the boys were away in school.

I was upstairs in my office, writing, when Naomi burst through the door, pale, wide-eyed, trembling. I looked at her and immediately said, "Is it one of the boys?"

She said, "Muddy," and she said, "The FedEx truck," and her sobs drowned out the rest of what she was trying to say.

I ran down the two flights of steps to the front door, and the FedEx driver was standing there, tears running down his cheeks. He said, "I'm sorry, I'm so sorry, I wasn't speeding." I saw Muddy in a pool of blood on the driveway about thirty yards away.

I started to run for her, the FedEx guy right next to me, and I saw the blood oozing from her head as we got nearer. I got down on the ground next to her and saw that her eyes were open and glassy and that she wasn't breathing. I felt the tears in my eyes then, too, and I leaned down and kissed her on her head and held her. The blood from her head was seeping in a stream to the grass. There was a lake of blood now around her body.

"I'm so sorry," the FedEx guy was mumbling, "I swear to you I wasn't speeding. She came out of nowhere." He didn't have to tell me that. Muddy had always had a bad habit of trying to round up cars, racing toward them, around them, and underneath them, and that's what had happened now. She'd raced for the FedEx truck she saw coming down the driveway and then gotten underneath it, and a piece of metal that stuck out from the undercarriage of the truck had struck her in the back of the head. It must have been like getting hit in the back of the head with a steel baseball bat.

"It's all right," I said to the driver, "I don't blame you." I told him about how Muddy had always tried to round vehicles up, but it didn't seem to console him. He was still crying.

"Will you say a prayer with me?" I asked the driver, and I kissed Muddy on the head again and started to say the Our Father. The driver was saying it with me. I held out my hand to him, and he took it and prayed with me. I saw Naomi standing at an upstairs window, watching us, crying.

When we finished our prayer, the driver and I picked Muddy up and moved her off the cement and onto the grass. The driver said, "Nothing like this has ever happened to me. I've been driving for fourteen years."

"It's okay," I said to him. "It is."

I shook his hand and he started away toward his truck.

I went into the house and held Naomi for a long time. I remembered the day Naomi had brought Muddy home from the pet store in Malibu. Naomi surprised me with her. We already had two other dogs and a newborn and two toddlers, and I said we couldn't really deal with another dog, so Naomi took her back to the pet shop that night. It was too late, of course. By then I'd seen her, and the next morning, bright and early, Naomi and I stood at the pet store door when it opened—hoping that Muddy would still be there.

When the kids got home from school on the day Muddy died, I told them what had happened. Joey was twelve; Lukey, our youngest, was five. All four of them started to cry. "We're getting a brand-new bulldog puppy tomorrow," I announced, and all four of them brightened. I knew from experience that the only way to cheer a child who'd lost a dog was to get another puppy just like the old one as soon as possible.

That night John Law, who was nine, asked me, "Why did God do this to Muddy?"

"God didn't do this," I said. "It was an accident."

"But God let it happen, didn't He?"

"Yes," I said, "but God will let me buy you a beautiful new puppy tomorrow."

We found a bulldog puppy on the Internet the next day and drove halfway across the state of Ohio early in the morning so that we'd have the new puppy when the kids got off the school bus.

So the boys went screwy when they saw him. He was cute — brown and white, with one brown paw and a black eye–like circle around one eye. We named him Pedro after the character in *Napoleon Dynamite.*

He was the dog from hell. He shat mountains all over the house. He threw up. He snarled at the boys. He ate the furniture. I joked a few weeks after we got him that while our house had eight thousand square feet of space, three thousand feet had already been eaten or defaced by Pedro. He quickly grew big and lumbering. He snored so loudly that our two cats, disturbed, howled all night. And he cut the smelliest farts of any dog I'd ever had, and I'd had a lot of dogs through the years. Not only did Pedro fart all the time, but he sought me out. He hunched down on the floor, his butt aimed at me, and he cut loose like a twin-barreled shotgun . . . *right at me.*

I started talking about getting rid of him. We decided to give it one more try. But nothing improved. He seemed to seek out my office to build his Alps of shit, and it seemed to me that at least five thousand square feet had been eaten or defaced by now, including the living room couches and the air hockey game down in the basement.

I had just about decided to pull the trigger on Pedro when Jesus saved him. I'm not kidding.

We had a small ceramic statue of Jesus in the backyard—the one that German television reporter had been so anxious to film—and one day Pedro's leash got tangled around it, and as Pedro galloped off, Jesus came crashing off the ledge we had Him on and broke into pieces.

I took it as a sign. Our ceramic Jesus had given His life for Pedro, so what right did I have to get rid of the damn dickhead dog? Six thousand square feet were gone now; there were Mount

Everests of shit to be constantly scooped in my office, in the basement, and in the den . . . and Pedro was happy—growing, growling, licking, biting, chewing, farting.

Our boys were happy, too, of course. They were Pedro's best pals, and they didn't have to clean it all up—we did.

Jesus said: Bless the beasts and the children.

He didn't say: Eff the beasts, bless the children.

*But* . . . the dog from hell, saved by Jesus, didn't act saved at all. He bounded down the road to perdition like a dumb, mad cow. He kept showing off his evil ways all over the house, sculpting brand-new fiendish turds that reeked like sulfur in hell. And he kept devouring the house, chewing away at the stairway now, gnawing at the very foundation of our home.

We couldn't take it anymore. There was a whole other way to view the demise of the ceramic Jesus statue, we now decided. We thought the Jesus statue had saved Pedro, but now we were thinking that Pedro had *killed* the Jesus statue.

We had misinterpreted God's sign.

Pedro had to go.

But still, we couldn't in good conscience countenance casting the hellish beast into hell: the local pound, Rescue Village, or Bulldog Rescue. We were too humanitarian, liberal, and suburban to do that. We'd been trying 24/7 to be good Christians, so to get any sleep we had to know that the dog from hell was "going to a good home."

Sharman, our vet, a no-BS biker lady soon to be off on a Harley roar across America, saved us this time. She found a couple in Solon (a town near us), a dentist and his wife, who already had one bulldog—a female named Napoleon who wanted company. Pedro, even though we'd already "fixed" him, would be an ideal companion for a female (he was silly, stupid, and bovine). Besides, Sharman told us, there was the most amazing coincidence: This bulldog named Napoleon had been named— you guessed it—from *Napoleon Dynamite,* too.

*That,* we knew (and never mind the shattered Jesus statue), was *definitely* a sign from God: Romeo and Juliet, both named from the same movie.

Pedro was history. We had our house back.

Even the hellish stink was gone.

ON OUR WAY to the ten o'clock Mass, Father Dan told me that a man he didn't know had been looking for me at the previous Mass.

The following weekend, as we were heading to the twelve o'clock Mass, Father Dan told me that the same man had been looking for me at the ten o'clock.

My boys at the same time told me that they kept seeing the same battered gray car driving up and down our street.

A couple of days later, I found the letter in my mailbox. It was handwritten, the words scrawled: "Dear Eszterhas, I need to talk to you about a matter of the greatest importance and privacy. Please call me at this number immediately." He signed his name. I didn't know the name; I'd never heard of him. There was a phone number and an address in Canton, Ohio, an industrial town south of Cleveland.

I had a policeman friend check him out. His name was Leo. He didn't have an arrest record, but he'd been in and out of psychiatric institutions in different parts of the country.

I called him and got his answering machine. I didn't want to be rude. I tried to be Christian about this. I left him a message: "Listen, Leo, this is Joe Eszterhas. If you keep following me around, I'm going to have you sent back to the loony bin. Good-bye. Have a good day and many God blesses and blessings."

The next day, Sunday, we went to the twelve o'clock Mass, and Father Dan caught me in the vestibule and said the same guy had been at the eight *and* the ten that morning, looking for me.

It was after Holy Communion. My head was down. My eyes were closed. I was focused on the body of Christ. I was lost in prayer. I felt a tap on my shoulder. I waved it off, thinking it was one of the boys wanting to know if we were stopping off for lunch at McDonald's or at Bob Evans. Then I felt the tap again, harder this time.

He looked to be in his mid-forties—bearded, long-haired, overweight, and short. He was dirty. He was beaming, holding something in his hand out to me. I couldn't believe what he was holding.

"I am Leo!" he whispered brightly. Then he said, "A script! For you! I brought it for you!"

"This is a church," I whispered. "I'm here praying to my God. You disturbed me with a *script* in church?"

"I am Leo!" he said. "It's a good script! My best! You can send it to your agent for me!"

People were looking at us. Some were still going to Communion. I noticed Naomi and the boys staring at this disheveled figure whispering to me. The boys looked scared.

I got up. I said, "Leo, listen to me." I put my arm around his neck and started walking him down the aisle out of church. He didn't resist. He stopped dead in the vestibule and tried to hand me the script. I kept my arm around his neck and dragged him outside.

"*Oww,*" he said, holding his neck. "That hurt. You hurt me!" He said it accusingly.

"Leo," I said, "are you listening to me?"

He looked at me suspiciously and nodded.

"Get the eff out of here!"

He said, "You said a bad word right outside the church!"

"You want me to say it again, Leo?"

"You're my inspiration," he said. "It's a courtroom drama like *Jagged Edge*. I've seen that movie six times."

I pushed him. I said, "Go! Now! Leave me the eff alone. If you bother me again, I'll call the cops—you hear me?" I pushed him again. He rubbed his shoulder where I'd touched him and just stared at me.

He held out the script. I took it and threw it at him. Pages went swirling everywhere.

"You get it now?" I said.

Leo said, "Fine! Fine! You know what? It's better than *Jagged Edge* anyway!" He started scampering around collecting the pages of his screenplay, mumbling under his breath.

I went back into the church and sat down next to Naomi and the boys just as Father Dan gave the blessing and said, "Go in peace to love and serve the Lord."

Leo was gone when we walked out of the church, but I saw one page of his screenplay caught in the bushes. I couldn't help myself. I read it when we got into the car.

I called him when we got home. I got his machine again. I said, "It is *not* better than *Jagged Edge*. But I read a page and it's not all that bad. Keep writing. And if you bother me again, I'm calling the cops."

I had gone in peace to love and serve the Lord.


THEY SAY that everyone who finds Jesus will be called upon to stand up for Him at some point in their lives . . . and I, who had been called a blasphemer and a pornographer, stood up for Him, too, and became His witness.

This is a Cleveland story, and in Cleveland you learn always to expect the unexpected, so my public witness—YOU GOTTA BE TOUGH, the T-shirts in Cleveland say—must be viewed in that Cleveland context. To wit: My witness for Jesus was about as unexpected as my onetime newspaper copyboy Dennis Kucinich (back in the day he shared his Beat poetry with me) becoming a candidate for president of the United States. To those who knew us both, Dennis's run for the White House made about as much sense as my witness for Jesus.

This is how it happened that I stood up for Jesus: He was my new pal. And I saw the hucksters and the unholy mocking Him, and I thought to myself: If Jesus came to my aid at my time of turmoil and trouble, then I will come to His aid now. Because they are mocking Him. And I couldn't stand by and let anyone mock my friend.

Not even . . . LeBron James.

*LeBron James?*

My favorite basketball player in the world?

Mocking Jesus?

*Says . . . who?*

Says me: Cleveland is an economically deprived city. Some say a dying city. A rusted-out, washed-up Rust Belt city. And when the Cleveland Cavaliers basketball team drafted LeBron James to play for them, there were those who said that LeBron, a nice, hardworking all-American type from the nearby city of Akron, practically a hometown boy, would be Cleveland's savior. The Cavs would sell out all their home games, the thinking went, and the money brought to the downtown area, thanks to LeBron, would save the city. I didn't have any problem with that or with LeBron—he would be my hometown's savior, with a small *s*.

No one was talking about capitalizing that letter to *S*.

Not yet.

But when LeBron started playing after he'd signed a gigantic megamillion-dollar deal with Nike, the shoe company, and a smaller megamillion-dollar deal with the Cavs, that small *s* in the word *savior* started to grow, as in the *Savior* . . . as in Jesus.

To begin with, Nike and the Cavs called him "the Chosen One." That had a familiar echo, especially when LeBron started calling himself "King James" (as in "the King James Bible"), which gave his self-chosen nickname a loud biblical ring. When the Cavs issued T-shirts that said, LEBRON—THE KING OF CLEVELAND, as in "Jesus of Nazareth, King of the Jews," that amped it to a deafening biblical ring. And, of course, the King James Bible talked a lot about "God's chosen people" and even made a reference to Jesus as "God's chosen one."

Then, in Nike's first LeBron commercials, he was shown flying through the air . . . *ascending,* if you will. Another ad showed the Chosen One bedecked in white robes in a Pentecostal church; angelic figures fluttered around him while the congregation hallelujaed and praised his glory.

I loved the way LeBron played basketball. I loved what he was doing for Cleveland, the city that I loved, and for the Cavs, the team that had broken my heart (along with the Indians and the Browns) during the thirty years I had lived in California.

But I couldn't—couldn't—just simply *couldn't*—stand there spacing out while everyone capital *S*'ed him into Our Savior.

I couldn't just stand by and do nothing while some fancy PR firm exploited Jesus to sell Nike shoes and Cavs tickets, doing their best to deify LeBron, transmogrifying a good, hardworking kid from Akron's ghetto . . . into a dunking, Nike-sporting, hometown Jesus . . . who *ascended* to the hoop and rattled heaven and earth with his almighty slam dunk. LeBron James had been re-created not by the Creator, but by the PR wizards: The kid from the ghetto was the Chosen One, the King of the Court, a mythical figure right out of the King James Bible who *appeared* in white robes in Pentecostal churches.

So . . . I went to war for my new friend Jesus against the forces of evil that had taken a poor ghetto kid and made him God. I felt like Joan of Arc fighting for my Lord. I felt like a wannabe martyr. I wasn't going to go chickenshit here like Peter. I felt like I was becoming my favorite Hungarian holy man, József Cardinal Mindszenty, who smacked down Nazis and Communists and his own Vatican and Richard Nixon, too. Well, I was going to smack down the Cavs and maybe Nike itself and the National Basketball Association and Commissioner David Stern, too.

I sat down at my old manual typewriter, greased it up, and fired away. I turned that typewriter into my own submachine gun, spewing out sentences and paragraphs of vitriol and fury. I wrote apoplectic, Howard Beale–influenced letters in protest of the exploitation of Jesus of Nazareth and the creation of our dunking hometown Jesus James. I sent letters to the Cavs and Nike and the NBA and David Stern and waited for the battle to be joined. And waited and waited and waited. Nothing. Not one letter back. No response. From anyone.

I started calling my friends, trying to stir up some grassroots support for the Lord. But my friends weren't interested in the Lord. They loved LeBron. They thought the Nike ads were cool. They thought LeBron had real acting talent. They were down at Quicken Loans Arena, watching him play. And they were already making plans to stir up grassroots support for Barack Obama: They didn't have any spare grassroots time left for Jesus.

I thought about showing up at the Q—which is what Clevelanders call Quicken Loans Arena—with a sign in my hand that said, LEBRON ISN'T JESUS. And Naomi said, "You're going to look like those kooks who are down at the Jake protesting Chief Wahoo at Indians games—is that what you want to be?" (Naomi used to be a public relations person specializing in damage control.) But Naomi was right. I didn't want to look like one of those crazed anti-Wahoo fanatics.

I gave up on my one-man pro-Jesus anti-LeBron protest and chickenshitted like Peter after all. I had to admit that I was a failure as Joan of Arc and József Cardinal Mindszenty; but how could I smack down the Cavs and Nike and the NBA and David Stern if they wouldn't even engage me?

I seethed, frustrated that I couldn't make my witness for Jesus—which was exactly the moment when the Cavs *really pissed me off*. They gave away (and then sold) simple black T-shirts with one word on them in big white letters: WITNESS. I wanted to be a witness for Jesus, and now there were thousands of people in Cleveland proclaiming themselves to be witnesses for their dunking *hometown* Jesus. Their cross was the Nike swoosh that they wore on the short sleeves of their black T-shirts.

This was blasphemy on the grandest scale: This wasn't just exploiting my Jesus, the redeemer of the world, anymore; this was conjuring an entirely new urban Jesus, a secular redeemer whose act of transfiguration was slamming it through the hole, whose sign of the cross was the three-pointer from the perimeter, whose blessing was the rosin he sprinkled onto his hands and then onto the crowd before the start of the games, whose eucharist was the sweated-out jersey he tossed into the crowd at the end of games.

Talk about the grandest scale: Nike erected a twenty-story billboard across the street from the Q. It showed LeBron in the act of transfiguration, above it the word WITNESS. The billboard was a shrine to LeBron, a massive Golgotha. Clevelanders gawked at it in awe, nearly crossing themselves, flashing cell phones in hand. As I watched them watching their dunking hometown Jesus one day at the Shrine of the Hoops Redeemer, I kept waiting for someone to genuflect.

I called my son Steve in Oregon, since he's one of the world's great basketball freaks.

I told Steve how upset I was. I told him that I thought this was horribly wrong—that Jesus, the real Jesus, the nondunking Jesus, shouldn't be exploited, satirized, and mocked this way.

"Hey, Pops," Steve said. "You know that French word they use when some movie steals a scene from another movie?"

*"Hommage?"*

"Yeah, that's it," Steve said. "That's what LeBron is doing here. He's not making fun of Jesus, he's paying tribute to him, doing *hommage*."

"That's cockeyed," I said.

"You gotta be a little bit more charitable, Pops," Steve said. "A little bit less judgmental. You know what I mean? Don't they teach you stuff like that in church?"

"You just love LeBron too much," I said to Steve. "It's because you ran into him at that restaurant in Portland and he signed that autograph for you. You told me he was a terrific, sweet guy. You're blind to what they're doing to Jesus in LeBron's name."

Steve said, "He *is* a terrific guy. But Pops, in basketball terms, he *is* Jesus. He is the NBA's messiah. He's not like one of these Jail Blazers we've got in Portland. He's got all-American values. He'll save the sport, he'll save Cleveland, and he'll save the Cavs."

Oh Lord, I almost hung up on my own son. *Father, forgive them, for they know not what they do. . . .* It was all my fault anyway with Steve, since he never heard anything about the real, undunking Jesus when he was growing up. I got him into sports but not into God. Back in the day, Steve's Jesus was Mark McGwire, the white-bread home-run-hitting saint of the Oakland A's.

But I still seethed. Oh, did I seethe! Nobody would listen to me. Not the Cavs, not Nike, not the NBA, not David Stern, not my friends, not my own beloved grown-up son. I greased the rickety manual typewriter and summoned the ghost of Howard Beale again. I submachine-gunned an article for the op-ed page of *The New York Times*. Rejected. I sent it to *The L.A. Times*. Rejected. To *Newsweek*. Rejected. To *The Cleveland Plain Dealer*, where I still had friends from the days I was employed there. But no. Rejected again! By my hometown newspaper!

Universally rejected, I was completely dejected.

And that's when the Cavs put out a new T-shirt, right in time for the NBA playoffs. In big letters, with LeBron's face in the background, the T-shirt said: THE RISING. You could have fooled me. It should have said: RESURRECTION FROM THE DEAD.

And then Nike changed the monstrous billboard across from the Q. On the new one, LeBron had both arms stretched out and raised to the heavens, his hands palms up to the sky and his head back, staring into the sky. It looked like he was ascending into heaven in a near crucifixion pose. Above it the new words said: WE ARE ALL WITNESSES.

I realized finally that there was no fighting this. For some people in Cleveland, the real Jesus was the new Jesus: LeBron James. I couldn't protect my new friend Jesus, redeemer of the world, no matter how desperately I wanted to. LeBron had eclipsed Him. Nike and the Cavs had pulled off the greatest identity theft in history.

*We adore thee, O Bron, and we bless thee, because by thy holy dunk thou hast redeemed the world!*

Led by their savior, the Cavs got into the NBA finals against the San Antonio Spurs. They lost four in a row. They were wiped out, demolished, decimated. There was no rising, no ascension into heaven.

The Chosen One was humiliated.

King James lost his crown.

The new Jesus wept.

My Jesus smiled.

We were all witnesses.

A few months later, LeBron, our hometown Jesus, went to a baseball playoff game at the Jake between the satanic New York Yankees and our beloved Cleveland Indians. LeBron wore a Yankees hat. He even told an interviewer how much he'd always loved the Yankees.

Clevelanders crucified him.

EVEN AT THE BEGINNING of the next basketball season, I couldn't stop seething about the Chosen One. The Cavs gave away rally towels for the Quicken Loans congregation that said: RISE UP! I got my towel at a game and watched as thirty-some thousand disciples hailed our dunking hometown Jesus's resurrection. I felt like I was attending the world's biggest biblical pep rally at the world's biggest megachurch, screaming at him, *"Rise up! Rise up! Rise up!"*

That Sunday, still seething, ready to erupt, I went to Mass at Holy Angels Church and sat there, slack-jawed, goo-goo-eyed, blood pressure thumping in my ears, as Deacon Fred touched on the same biblical theme in his homily.

"Did you hear?" Deacon Fred bellowed. "Did you hear what happened? Did you hear the news?

"A group of young boys were gathered at an inner-city playground playing basketball last weekend. And as they did every Saturday, these young boys raced back and forth, back and forth, calling their own fouls, lost in the game.

"But this Saturday was different. Very different. Very, very different. This Saturday a car drove up. A car drove up and a man got out. He was tall. Very tall, very, very tall—three times the size of most of the boys. *Tall!* And as he neared them and called for the ball, they realized who it was.

"It was him! It was the King. It was the Chosen One. Did you hear? Did you hear what happened? Did you hear the news?

"And as LeBron James moved among them, they stood there in awe—*awe!*—hanging on his every word, watching his every move, witnessing. Witnessing the miracle! Witnessing it! *Witnessing* it!

"The news spread quickly that the Chosen One had walked among us. The Chosen One was here! And an excitement rose as the buzz of his arrival spread through the neighborhood and then onto the next neighborhood and then onto the neighborhood after that and then onto the suburbs and then onto the next town and the next and the next until it reached the news on television and the front page of the newspaper!

"He was here! The Chosen One! He walked among us! Did you hear? Did you hear what happened? Did you hear the news?

"And as I contemplated those events, those miraculous events, I thought about how it must have been when Cheeze-us chose to walk among us. How the word must have spread through the neighborhood and then onto the next neighborhood and then onto the neighborhood after that and then onto the suburbs and then onto the next town and the next and the next. *Cheeze-us!* Cheeze-us among us! Cheeze-us among us! How the word must have spread! How the excitement built with each sighting! How they must have said, 'Did you hear? Did you hear what happened? Did you hear the news? The Chosen One has arrived! Cheeze-us! Cheeze-us among us!'

"And as we lead our lives, we must remember that Cheeze-us still walks among us. In a good deed, in a kind word, in an act of kindness. We see Him! The Chosen One! Cheeze-us! He walks among us and shows us the way. The way and the truth. The way and the truth and the life. Cheeze-us! We witness His miracle! We are all witnesses! *Witnesses!* Witnesses for Cheeze-us!"

On my way home, I resolved that next Sunday I was going to bring my Cavs rally towel to Mass instead of my rosary. And they would say: "Did you hear? Did you hear what happened? Did you hear the news? He strangled Deacon Fred with it. Right there in church!"


I WAS IN A JAM with my book publisher. Before I was saved, I had made a deal with my publisher to write a dark mystery about a series of killings. The novel was to be called *The Fun,* and at its center were a husband and wife who killed cheap women in Vegas together after seducing them together and having sex with them. Thrill killing had taken the place of their sexual climax; thrill killing was their "fun." On the surface, they were an all-American couple, churchgoing midwesterners, the parents of two little kids. He was a cop; she was a working soccer mom.

I had been paid a large amount of up-front money to write the book, and my publisher was anxious that I write and finish it as soon as possible. He thought it was possible it would become a worldwide bestseller. The book's jacket would feature the line "From the author of *Basic Instinct* and *Jagged Edge.*"

The book was to be the same kind of dark, twisted sexual thriller that I had become famous for; it was to be, at its core, as *Basic Instinct* had been, about evil and the nature of evil. And, as in *Basic Instinct,* at the book's end, the couple would get away with the crimes. The killings and their fun would continue . . . just as Catherine Tramell in *Basic Instinct,* at the end of the film, was living happily ever after with her ice pick under the bed, ready for more whenever she so chose.

It was what had driven the actor Michael Douglas, no fan of mine, so crazy about the movie he'd starred in. "You can't end the movie this way," he had said to me. "Evil triumphs. That's wrong. That's the statement that you want to make? That evil triumphs?"

So . . . after being saved . . . after becoming a crossbearer at Holy Angels Church . . . after moving away from Hollywood and living in Ohio . . . it was time for me now to become "the king of the icepicks" again.

It was time to write *The Fun.*

*But* . . . I couldn't do it. I tried. I sat at my desk for months and tried. I got it started, but then I had to stop. *I just couldn't do it!* Not because of any withdrawal from cigarettes and alcohol. I was able to write whatever else I wanted to write now . . . but not *The Fun.*

I had been *saved!* My head was in a bright, positive, loving place. A good, not an evil, place. I couldn't force myself to go back into the dark world I'd explored creatively for so many years, that neon-lit black velvet wonderland populated by hookers and demons who fornicated and pranced through streets smeared with blood and hair.

I couldn't force myself to stand in the shoes of human beings who had "fun," who got off killing other human beings.

I didn't want to depict churchgoing midwesterners, my

neighbors, as sick monsters who camouflaged their evil with flags, crosses, and family values.

That wasn't, to use Michael Douglas's words, "the statement" I wanted to make anymore. If, as some said, *Basic Instinct,* more than any other movie, glamorized both evil and smoking, then maybe my throat cancer was the price I'd paid for glamorizing both.

If anything, I now wanted to glamorize the goodness and the redemptive possibilities in man. After all these years, I was ready to agree with Michael Douglas and say to him: "You were right, man, I should have listened to you."

The man who was trying but failing to write *The Fun* wasn't the same man who'd made the deal to write it. God's presence was in his heart, and he knew now that you can't write blood and hair on the walls with God in your heart.

So I stopped trying to force it and wrote another book instead of *The Fun,* a semisatirical screenwriting primer that made people laugh and . . . have "fun." And I even advised screenwriters that it was okay to say a prayer before they began writing.

My publisher wasn't amused when he heard he wasn't getting *The Fun.* He threatened lawsuits. He threatened to tie me up in court for years. But I couldn't write the damn book. I'd tried, but God wouldn't let me.

HE WAS COMING THIS SUNDAY, after the noon Mass. Our church pews were abuzz with excitement.

He was a healer, a "miracle man." He laid his hands on you, and by his touch he cured you of your afflictions. It was whispered that he was God's instrument, a creature of the Holy Spirit.

It was said he had cured so many of the Afflicted that the

diocese had recently allowed him to perform his miracles in church, after Mass. He had somehow, miraculously, chosen our little church, Holy Angels, for his next appearance. The Afflicted from as far away as Illinois and Michigan—Minnesota, even— had e-mailed that they were coming to be touched by him.

I was one of the Afflicted. My throat cancer was in remission, but if this man could *cure* me, then I wanted him to touch me. I signed my name on the official list of the Afflicted who wanted to be touched. I was given a number. I was number twenty-three. This meant that I would be touched in the first hour of healing, I wouldn't have to stand around for hours. My low number—it was Michael Jordan's number; LeBron James's number as well—was God's blessing. There would be those who would have to wait twelve hours for their miracles.

We went to the noon Mass that Sunday—Naomi, our four boys, and I, eager to be touched, to be cured of my affliction. There were wheelchairs everywhere in church as the noon Mass ended. A blind man sat in the pew in front of us with his wife. The keening jibber-jabber of handicapped children filled the air.

Rubber mats had been placed on the floor in front of the altar. They looked somehow sinister there, as though they had been swiped from a hospital supply closet. I asked someone what they were for. "When he touches someone," I was told, "they often faint." The thick rubber mats were there to protect those who would fall. They were called "miracle mats."

The Healer arrived. He was accompanied by his wife, his teenage daughter, and his assistants. There were about a dozen assistants. They had headsets plugged into their ears, their mikes framing their faces. They were young men and women in their twenties and thirties, stylishly dressed. They looked a little like

Secret Service agents but more like the efficient, harried assistants to Hollywood agents. The Healer's top assistant, his administrative aide, was a well-known local disk jockey. He spoke like a disk jockey cliché, even here at the healing. "Okay, folks, we'll be getting going now in a couple minutes," he said, "so let's start lining up in front of the miracle mats here in front of the altar. Okay, let's go for it!"

The Healer was standing on a miracle mat. He was a nondescript, slouchy, pasty-faced man in his late forties, a little on the pudgy side. He wore brown slacks and brown shoes, a white shirt and brown tie. Father Dan introduced him to me. He had a fish handshake. His palm was pudgy and wet. His gaze didn't meet mine. He said nothing. He turned quickly away to shake someone else's hand. I kept trying to figure out who he reminded me of, and then it came to me. Peter Sellers. Peter Sellers as Chauncey Gardner in *Being There.* I remembered reading that the Healer was Lebanese.

The Healer's wife—also in her forties—was Romanian. She had deep-set, dark, and hungry eyes. She looked me deep in the eye when she shook my hand.

She said, "You sick?"

I said yes.

She said, "He help you."

I said, "Great."

She said suspiciously, "You no believe?"

I said I didn't know.

She nodded, smiled, and turned quickly away to shake hands with someone else, too.

The healing began. The disk jockey called out, "Pray for the miracle! Pray to Jesus!" The Afflicted began shuffling toward their miracle mats.

The Healer went from one person to the other, from one miracle to the other. He touched the Afflicteds' heads, necks, and shoulders. Four of his headsetted assistants held the Afflicted from all sides to make sure they didn't fall when they fainted.

The Healer mumbled prayers for each person, but so quietly we couldn't hear what he was saying or what language he was speaking—English? Arabic? Romanian? Each healing took about a minute. No one fainted. No one fell to a miracle mat. One old lady swooned demurely.

Now it was my turn. *"Number twenty-three!"* The disk jockey announced it like I'd won the lottery, scored a touchdown, or shot a goallllllllllllllll! My rubber miracle mat was empty, waiting for me. The four assistants were standing there, speaking softly into their headsets. In my mind I could hear the disk jockey's bellowing carny voice: "Step right up! Step right up here, folks, for your own true-blue miracle."

I didn't want to go up there. I didn't want to stand on the miracle mat. I didn't want those headsetting agents' assistants holding me. I didn't want Peter Sellers or Chauncey Gardner babbling at me under his breath in Arabic or Romanian or even English. I didn't want his slimy hands on me.

I felt sudden rage. I loved God. I believed in miracles. I was grateful for His presence in my life. But in my opinion this pudgy, pasty-faced weasel was mocking God. His so-called miracles were a geek's sideshow; the disk jockey welcomed you into the tent where the three-breasted fat lady sat. Diocesan officials who'd allowed this freak show to take place in church—*in front of the altar!*—should have been handcuffed to their pedophile brothers and condemned to eternally molest one another in hell.

I leaned over to Naomi and said, "Let's get out of here!" I got up, and Naomi and the boys followed me out of our little church. I saw the Healer's wife glaring at me as we left.

On the way to our car, we passed the Healer's teenage daughter. She was sitting on the sidewalk, her cell phone in hand, having a loud argument with her boyfriend. *In English.*

A week or so later, *The Plain Dealer,* our local newspaper, wrote an article about the Healer's miracles. It seemed the Healer wasn't just a healer—he was an acupuncturist, too. His acupuncturist practice was booming. Many of the Afflicted who attended his healings were calling him later for a private appointment, a *private* acupuncture healing. The appointments were expensive, and the Healer was booked far in advance, although a woman who was dying called and was told the Healer would see her right away, at midnight in his office. All she had to do was bring two hundred dollars for her miracle. In cash. She went to his office at midnight. She paid him the two hundred dollars for her miracle. In cash. She died days later.

We went to a Minor League baseball game later that summer in Eastlake, a Cleveland suburb where the Lake County Captains were playing. The young woman who sang the national anthem looked familiar to me. She was a local celebrity, we were told. Then I placed her. The Healer's daughter sang the anthem beautifully.

FATHER DAN DISAGREED WITH ME about the Healer.

A woman with breast cancer, Father Dan said, went to see the Healer. And after she saw him, she went back to her doctors. Her doctors reexamined her and said there was a growth in her breast but it was no longer cancerous.

A man went to see the Healer, Father Dan said, who hadn't been able to turn his head from side to side in years. On his way back from his miracle mat to his pew, his wife noticed that the man was looking around the church, his head moving perfectly.

Then Father Dan talked about a little girl who went to see the Healer at Holy Angels with her parents. As her parents prepared to leave, the little girl said "We can't go. I see Jesus here."

"God chooses the most unlikely subjects to preach the word of God," Father Dan said. "Look at John the Baptist. He was eating locusts and honey in the desert and he was chosen to spread word that the Savior was coming."

Father Dan gave me a look. He saw that I was still unconvinced that the Healer was a man of God.

Father Dan said, "If God can choose Joe Eszterhas to spread the word of God, then why not the Healer?"

There was no way I could argue with that.

I KNEW that I had seen one real medical miracle with my own eyes, many years ago.

My father had a heart valve replacement at the age of eighty-five and, owing to complications, had to have four other subsequent major surgeries immediately afterward. Three months after the initial surgery, he was still in the intensive care unit. He was barely alive, in and out of a coma.

One night when I went to see him, they had him strapped into some kind of machine to help his circulation. He was elevated high in the air. It was like he was hanging up there above me on an X-shaped cross.

I stood at the foot of my father's cross watching his head loll, and I suddenly became aware that someone was standing next to me. It was a white-haired doctor in his sixties.

"Is this your dad?" he asked.

I nodded. He didn't look at me. His eyes were fixed on my father's X-shaped cross.

"Your father has no business being alive," the doctor said. "He should have died twenty times in the last week alone. I've never believed in miracles before, but I do now."

My father left the intensive care unit two months later. He lived another nine years, until the age of ninety-four.

I HAD GOTTEN LETTERS through the mail for many years from screenwriters begging me to read their scripts. I had refused everyone: My lawyers had impressed me with the fact that if I read other writers' screenplays, they could sue me in the future for writing something myself that they claimed was influenced by what they'd sent me.

But now I was trying to be a good Christian, and after I finished the most recent letter from a struggling screenwriter, I was tempted to defy my lawyers.

His name was Vince. He had written a script that he begged me to read. He lived in Strongsville, a middle-class suburb on the West Side of Cleveland. This is part of the letter Vince wrote me:

"I'm not a refugee from Hungary. I'm a 'reb-u-gee' from the South. I never had real roots. In 1997, I made my way to Ohio. Looking for companionship, I eventually put a personal ad on the Internet that consisted of seven adjectives. I got two responses. The first was from a woman who was only writing to inform me that I would be alone the rest of my life. The second was from a Serbian woman who would become my wife on the first day of 1998 and we commenced making children. That ad was the best thing I ever wrote and every day I am grateful for the profit it brings. I can only imagine the requests you've had to read scripts. Everyone has a sob story. I don't know what might move you to agree to read one of mine, but I doubt it will be pity. I could try the pity route and tell you about my youngest daughter. She was diagnosed this past October with Type 1 diabetes. But the fact is that she is more than capable of handling this disease. At the age of seven, she has taken control of it, even administering (under close supervision, of course) her own injections. But you can't find pity there. Only admiration. She's the strongest, bravest person I know. My seven-year-old daughter is my hero. So much for pity."

I called one of my lawyer friends in Beverly Hills and told him I was thinking about responding to a letter and reading a script. He said, "You can't do that, you'll get sued."

I said, "What if I don't?"

He said, "You will. And even if you don't, you'll worry constantly about being sued and that will affect your happiness and your work."

I said, "What if the script is brilliant and this guy just needs a helping hand to live his life?"

My lawyer friend laughed. "As far as I know, you're not a social worker, right? Besides, the script will suck. Every script out there without an agent behind it sucks. If the guy was any good, he'd have an agent. He wouldn't have to go begging you to read the shit he created."

A harsh, cynical Hollywood assessment, I thought—definitely an un-Christian one, although the chances were good that my lawyer friend was right on the money with his assessment of Vince's script.

I thought about what he had told me, and I was happy that he was my lawyer. It was that kind of protection that I wanted.

Then I called Vince.

He said, "Hello?" in a timid kind of way. I recognized the

southern drawl right away. There was a lot of noise in the background. It sounded like kids yelling at one another—not all that different from the noise in the background when someone called me.

I said, "Hi, this is Joe Eszterhas."

There was an endless pause. I thought he had hung up or that we had somehow been disconnected.

Finally, very quietly, he said, "Yessir?"

I said, "I'll read your script."

He said, "Yessir," again the same way.

I said, "I'll give you where to send it. You got a pencil?"

He said, "Yessir."

I gave him my address. He wrote it down. He said, "Thank you, sir," and hung up on me.

You schmuck, I said to myself. You've gone and really done it now, you've given this weird stranger your home address— where your wife and little boys, the people you love most in the world—live. This guy is obviously some kind of psycho— *Yessir, yessir, yessir, yessir.* You've developed some kind of suicidal Christ complex. This guy's not going to sue you, he'll probably come over and ice pick you. You'll be responsible for the death of your whole family! How's that for being a good Christian?

The script came the next day by FedEx. When I saw the title, my worst fears were confirmed—*A Walk in Hell on Sunday.* Oh God! No doubt now that he was a nut job. "Hell" and "Sunday" together in the same title. Some kind of religious maniac, probably. Some poor guy like Bobby, my late brother-in-law, trapped between the devil ("Hell") and God ("Sunday"). I remembered how I had to move my family to Hawaii for a while when Bobby was supposedly on his way to kill me. Where *in the hell* would we move to when Vince was on *his* way with *his* guns? Amelia Island? Hilton Head? Longboat Key? Some other East Coast vacation resort ideal to hide in?

I read his script. I couldn't put it down. It was brilliant. Set in the South, it was about blacks and whites trying to make sense of each other. It was raw and powerful. I couldn't believe it. I was flabbergasted. I was overwhelmed.

I called Vince as soon as I finished it.

"Vince," I said.

He said, "Yessir."

I said, "You recognized my voice."

"Nosir, you're the only person I know where the phone says 'Private' instead of a number."

"Your script is brilliant. I loved it."

"Yeah," he said, "thank you, sir, but it's not my most commercial script, I know. I've got another one, though, that's real commercial. Can I send that to you, too, sir?"

How could I possibly say no? I'd just read a script that had knocked me out and now he was offering me a chance to read another one. I'd had so much fun reading the first one.

I told him to send the other script, which he said was called *Or Else*.

"One thing, though, Vince."

He said, "Yessir."

"Please don't call me 'sir' anymore. Call me Joe."

"Yessir," he said.

I got *Or Else* the next day and read it right away, and he was right. It was more commercial than *A Walk in Hell on Sunday*. But just as powerful. Vince was a talented man.

I called him back and told him how much I loved this script, too, and asked him if he could come to my house the next day. I wanted to meet him.

"You tell me where and when and I'll be there, sir," he said. "Joe," he corrected himself. "I'll be there, Joe."

He was there at ten in the morning, not a minute early, not a minute late. He was forty years old. He had longish auburn hair. He was a good-looking man—big and tall—a few pounds too heavy. He had a soft shyness and a charming southern manner.

I told him how talented I thought he was. I told him I wanted to send both scripts, with his permission, to big-name Hollywood producers I knew, trusted, and had worked with.

He sat there not saying anything for some time. His eyes were glancing around the walls of my den at all my movie posters displayed there. Then his eyes held mine and he said, "I'm sorry, sir— Joe, I just don't know how to respond. I read all your books and I've seen all sixteen of your movies. I know exactly who you are. And I can't believe I'm sitting here in your den talking to you. And I can't believe that you like my work and think I'm talented. And I can't believe that you're going to send my scripts to some producers. I've just gotta take a minute to let all this sink in!" He sat there, looking down, almost hulked into himself. He suddenly said, "Wow," and shook his head. And he said, "Oh, my God, man!" and he started to laugh. I laughed with him and I put my hand up in the air and gave him a high five. He slapped my hand hard.

I liked him. Vince was easy to like. He had grown up in the South. His mom and dad had both been alcoholics. He had worked an endless series of very odd jobs—he'd even been a policeman for a while. He was working for a title company now, trying to make ends meet. He had three kids and he wrote mostly at night, when his wife and kids were asleep. He'd always loved to write, although he was relatively uneducated. He began with short stories, then wrote graphic novels, and was now writing screenplays. He loved movies and he knew a lot about them.

As he left my house after our first meeting, he said, "I don't know how to thank you. I'll never know how to thank you. I'm not sure you know what this means. If nothing comes of all this—if nobody else likes my scripts—you've already changed my life. You've already given me the encouragement that will keep me writing. I've never had any encouragement before except for my wife, let alone from anybody like you."

I sent *Or Else* to my producer friend David, who sent it on to Renny Harlin, a well-known Hollywood director who had done *Cliffhanger* and *Die Hard 2*. Renny loved Vince's script, attached himself to it, and said it would be his next film.

I sent *A Walk in Hell on Sunday* to my producer friend Craig, who sent it to Oscar-winning producer Cathy Schulman (*Crash*), who sent it on to actor-director Don Cheadle. We were waiting for Don to read it, but Cathy felt that even if Cheadle didn't direct it himself, he'd love the script and send it on to one of his director friends.

Vince was going to be a Hollywood screenwriter. He wouldn't have to paint houses anymore. He would be able to take care of the wife and kids that he loved. He'd have to worry less about his diabetic daughter. I *had* changed his life. I *was* being a good Christian. I felt Father Jack Turek, Father Dan, and Father Bob patting me on the back.

I called my lawyer friend and told him what was going on with both of Vince's scripts.

"Isn't that fantastic?" I said. "You see—you were too cynical. The scripts are brilliant, the guy isn't a mass murderer, and I'm not going to get sued."

"What do you get out of this?"

"What do you mean?"

"You discovered him, you should be a producer on his movies."

"I don't know anything about producing."

"Nobody knows anything about producing. You can learn. You know as much as the next guy."

"I didn't do this so I could be a producer."

"You did it for some wild-ass reason I'll never understand," my lawyer friend said. "What you did was stupid and could have endangered you both financially and physically. But Joe—now that you did it, now that both scripts are going to be movies, you should be credited and paid as a producer."

I called Vince and asked him how he'd feel about me being a producer on his films with David and Craig. Vince said, "Joe, if you asked me for my left nut right now, I'd give it to you. Both nuts. You want 'em, you got 'em."

I had two thoughts when I hung up:

1. Vince would survive in Hollywood.

2. Being a good Christian could really pay off.

*But* . . . as it so often happens in Hollywood, everything unraveled, the center would not hold.

Renny Harlin sent *Or Else* to his agent for another read. The agent didn't like the script, and Renny said he was sorry, but he was considering other scripts to direct next. He might direct it *after* his next film if the right deal came along.

Don Cheadle, busy in preproduction with a Miles Davis movie, never even read *A Walk in Hell on Sunday*. Craig kept waiting for an answer from him, never got one, and soon he had to start all over again. He began the exhausting process of sending the script to other directors.

Vince was trying his best not to let the fact that we basically had to start all over again with both projects get to him. But he had mouths to feed and, feeling like he had been that close to grabbing the brass ring, soon had to join a weekend house-painting crew to pay the bills.

I hoped that by trying to help him, by trying to be a good Christian, I hadn't broken his heart.

JACK NICHOLSON WAS THE GUY he usually hung out with. He played golf with Jack and smoked dope with Jack and they scored a lot of action together. Jack called him Loody. He was a former film director, a sometime producer, though now, in his sixties, he was mostly a philanthropist. He was a fixer, really. Billionaires used him to negotiate deals for resorts and hotels that they wanted to own.

I'd always liked him, but I hadn't seen him in years. We used to hang out together in the final years of my first marriage, drinking together, doing the same things he and Jack were now doing together. Having fun. Loody was a good-time guy and so was I, and we had a good time together.

I hadn't heard from him or seen him since the newspapers reported that I had throat cancer. I hadn't expected to. Loody was a good-time guy. Cancer isn't a good time.

Six years after my surgery, six years after I'd last heard from him, I ran into Loody during an L.A. visit. I had gone to church on Sunday in Beverly Hills with Naomi. We were sitting there waiting for Mass to begin when Loody walked in. I watched him as he came in. He looked good. In shape. A little pumped, even. He had to be in his late sixties.

I couldn't believe he was in church. Loody? Loody the good-time guy? Loody the life of the party? *In church? In God's house?* I looked again to make sure I was seeing right.

Yup, it was Loody!

Then he saw me sitting there with Naomi. He stared. He gaped. His jaw dropped. He almost dropped his drawers. *Me? In church?* Good-time Joey (his nickname for me)? Joey the boozer, the carouser, the cocksman? *In church? In God's house?* Loody lowered his glasses. I knew what he was doing. He was checking to see if it was really me. Then his eyes shifted to Naomi.

Yup, it was me all right.

He took a couple of fast steps toward me, and I got up quickly from the pew and took a couple of fast steps toward him, and we hugged. We babbled the things Hollywood people babble to each other when they haven't seen each other for a while. *You look great. . . . How are ya. . . . God, it's great to see you, . . . You look fantastic. . . . You haven't changed at all.*

And suddenly the choir burst into song. The procession started coming down the aisle toward us. Loody and I sat back down quickly and whispered that we'd see each other after Mass.

I noted, as the young priest came down the aisle, that he knew Loody. The priest bowed a little toward him as he passed him, and Loody bowed back. He was a young Indian priest, I discovered during the homily, who'd been assigned to this parish for a year. This was his last Mass. He was flying to Europe that afternoon.

When the Mass ended, Loody and I hugged again, and the three of us headed to the back of the church. I asked how he'd been, and he said he was producing a play on Broadway and was having trouble with the writer—*so what else was new?* He asked how I'd been, and I said I was fine—six years in remission, and my throat, as he heard, was now a cancer-free healthy croak.

"I'll say a prayer for you," Loody said. I smiled and thanked him.

The young priest was there, and Loody said, "Father, I've set your limo up for you for two o'clock. I'll ride to the airport with you." The young priest smiled and patted Loody on the back and thanked him.

Loody introduced me to the priest and said I had throat cancer. "Father, can I ask you for a favor?" Loody said. "Can I ask
you to bless my friend Joey?"

The priest stepped closer to me and held my throat with
both of his hands and, looking straight into my eyes, said some
prayers, never taking his eyes off mine. Then he brought me
closer to him, kissed me on the forehead, and hugged me. And
all the time he was praying, Naomi held me by one hand and
Loody held me by the other.

I was moved; I thanked the priest and thanked Loody and
hugged him. Loody handed me an Our Lady of Guadalupe holy
card and told me again that he'd pray for me. Then he whispered, "I love ya," in the old clichéd Hollywood way, and was
gone.

I felt like I'd dreamed all of it. *Loody in church. Loody holding
my hand during a blessing. Loody saying he'd pray for me. Loody hand-
ing me a holy card.*

All of that made about as much sense as *me being in church, me
being blessed, me having my hand held, me taking the holy card, me
putting it carefully away.*

Loody called me a few months later. He had hooked up
with a new company that wanted to fund movies. And he had
an idea he wanted me to write. It was the story of the DEA—
the Drug Enforcement Administration—and its battle against
drugs.

I was interested. I admired what the DEA was doing. They
were trying to save my four boys, and millions of others, from
being damaged by drugs. They risked their lives in an endless
bloody battle against the forces of evil. They were more than
just good guys. They were heroes.

Loody flew Naomi and me from Cleveland to L.A., first
class, put us up in a lavish suite at a Beverly Hills hotel, and set

up meetings both with DEA agents and with Orin, the head of the financing company.

My meetings went well and, remarkably, I found myself (in Hollywood terms) in unfamiliar company, because the DEA people and Orin were people of faith. I found myself talking about God with them, and they told me how important God was in their lives. Orin's pastor drove up from Orange County to meet me, and I found myself holding hands with him and praying in the dining room of our hotel as everyone stared.

And Loody amazed me. A lifelong Hollywood animal, he talked constantly about his devotion to Our Lady of Guadalupe. Loody knew the story in great detail—how the Virgin appeared to the peasant Juan Diego, and how her appearance converted the nation of Mexico only a few years after the Aztecs were killing twenty thousand people a day in sacrifices for the sun god. We had to have another meeting with DEA officials at La Quinta, outside Palm Springs, and as we got into town, Loody told us about a beautiful church he had discovered here. We stopped. St. Francis of Assisi was closed, but we found an open back door and went into the dark church to say a few prayers. The church was stunning, done in the old Mission style, and I watched Loody as he put both hands on an Our Lady of Guadalupe mural and leaned against it in prayer, channeling its power and grace.

Our meeting with the DEA officials was successful. They approved our project. I was happy. I would get a chance to write a script about good guys who fight a heroic war to save our children. It seemed a long way from *Basic Instinct* and *Showgirls*.

On the way back to L.A., I told Loody that I wanted to write a film someday about Our Lady of Guadalupe. "A small film," I said, "with a low budget. If we do it right, it could be like a prayer. I'll write the script for nothing."

"Let's do it," Loody says. "It will be our legacy."

We had a meeting in L.A. with Orin, who would finance the DEA movie. It was a short meeting.

"Let's do it," Orin said. "Let's get going."

Loody brought up the movie about Our Lady of Guadalupe, and Orin thought about it and said, "Fine. We'll do that, too. Keep the budget to five million. We can do that."

As we left, Orin hugged me and said, "You are a real blessing."

And so it happened that in Hollywood, a godless place, the head of a film finance company gave a screenwriter a hug and called him a blessing.

And so it happened that in Hollywood, the king of sex and violence, a man who'd often been called a misogynist and a sexist, made a deal to write the story of Our Lady of Guadalupe.

None of it would have happened had two sinners not run into each other "accidentally" in church.

I WAS GOING TO WRITE THE SCRIPT about Our Lady of Guadalupe as a very special gift to my mother, who had always revered the Blessed Virgin.

I remembered that when I was a boy, my mother had told me to turn to the Virgin (and Saint Anthony of Padua, of all people) whenever I needed help. "God's too busy with too many things for me to bother Him," my mother had said. "But He's never too busy to listen to His mother." During the Marian years, years that the pope dedicated to the Blessed Virgin, my mother tried to go to Mass every morning. She prayed at the Blessed Virgin's side altar in any church she attended.

Naomi and Loody had the same kind of die-hard devotion to the Blessed Virgin. I saw Loody go off like a rocket when a nondenominational, Jesus-centric preacher scoffed at the notion of praying to Mary. Loody got up and left the table. "Could you believe that dumb SOB," he said later, "that silly A-hole. Who the eff does he think he is to put down the Blessed Virgin Mary?" Loody said the Virgin "has never turned me down with anything that I've ever asked of her."

I, on the other hand, had never had an easy time fitting the Blessed Virgin into my personal pantheon. I had been a young and priapic man, and I couldn't accept the proposition that the Holy Spirit, let alone some anonymous archangel, had impregnated Mary. Or, closer to the bone, impregnating Mary *and then saying that there was no sex*. It had always seemed to me that, minimally, Spirit or archangel, there was sex.

Now, however, I finally understood the concepts of the Immaculate Conception and the Virgin Birth. It was all about faith. If you believed that God made man . . . if you believed that God sent His beloved Son to redeem man . . . that Jesus died and was resurrected and went to heaven . . . then it was easy to believe in a sexless, G-rated Immaculate Conception and a Virgin Birth shot in soft focus with gauzy lens.

And I did believe it.

Besides that, there were several aspects of the Guadalupe apparitions that were mind-boggling to me. The cloak that had been left with the Virgin's picture on it was examined by atheistic scientists who had no explanation for what was there. A Nobel Prize–winning, self-described atheist, the German chemist Richard Kuhn, said: "The elements that produced the colored patches on the cloth are unknown to all research. Neither mineral, animal, nor vegetable, the image seems to have been painted without any brush strokes or lithographic method." Kuhn admitted that he had looked forward to exposing the Guadalupe apparitions as a world-renowned fraud before he examined the cloak and the picture. Another team of American scientists said in 1946 that "if the image of the woman on the cloth had been hand-made, it could only have been made by techniques unknown by artists or scientists of the twentieth century." (The cloak had been left in 1531.)

Kuhn was an atheist as witness to the supernatural. He wanted to expose La Virgen as a phony. But his honesty overcame his atheism. This was Dick Cheney saying the war in Iraq was a fraud, Pat Robertson saying that Bill Clinton was a great president, me saying that UFOs were real.

What I particularly liked about the picture of La Virgen itself was that she was standing on a serpent, vanquishing it, defeating evil. I was supersensitive to the existence of serpents in the world, of course, because we had so many of them lurking where we lived, in the shadows of the Wetlands in Bainbridge Township. I couldn't forget, either, how one damn ugly serpent had gone after Naomi on a damp summer day. An icon of a woman standing on a serpent was yet one more icon I wanted on the walls of our house, along with the crosses, the grinning Chief Wahoos, and the Rolling Stones tongues.

I liked the *strength* that La Virgen conveyed by standing atop the serpent's head. I'd always been attracted to strong women; Naomi was one of the strongest women I'd ever met, and I'd created several strong leading women in my films—in *Jagged Edge, Betrayed, Music Box, Basic Instinct,* and *Showgirls.* All strong women, though admittedly not virginal or immaculate. But then the women I'd created came from my febrile, priapic, non-virginal, and exceedingly maculate imagination. And while my women were indeed strong, none of them was strong enough to stand on top of the head of the Serpent himself. The truth was that many of them (think Sharon Stone and Elizabeth Berkley) would probably have tried to seduce the Serpent instead of vanquishing him.

Loody was already planning a trip to Mexico City to see La Virgen at her basilica, and there was some talk that we'd combine the holy trip with our DEA project. We'd go down to Mexico to see the drug wars firsthand with the DEA guys and go off to the basilica during breaks in the gunfire.

I viewed my belief in La Virgen as a natural part of my spiritual progression: First I believed in UFOs. Then I was saved and believed in God. Then I had my head turned by La Virgen, although I still didn't believe in holy or unholy angels.

I didn't yet believe in Saint Anthony of Padua, either, but I didn't rule him out. I knew I had to do some serious reading about him. I had to find out what had so mesmerized my mother about a bald little Franciscan with a potbelly who had a knack for finding things.


THERE WAS a God almighty chattering in the pews and in the vestibule, in the basement and in the chapel—even in the vast, brightly lighted parking lot!—of Holy Angels Church.

Big, big news! Not as apocalyptic maybe as the tsunami of events that had led to the allegations, according to *The Plain Dealer*, that founding Father Joe was a "child sex abuser," but certainly bigger news than the revelation that corned beef and cabbage—and pierogis!—would be added to the Lenten fish fry menu.

It was unbelievable but true: We would be getting another priest at Holy Angels!

He would assist Father Dan, whose heroic commitment to his stewardship was stressing him out so badly that he was rapidly losing most of the little hair he had left atop his head. Father Dan was so busy that he hardly had any time at all to himself, not even to watch the Food Network on television that he loved so much. He looked exhausted. On certain Sundays he had *satchels* under his eyes. His usually ruddy complexion was sometimes a waxy grayish white. All those many Masses! All those many funerals! All those endless weddings, baptisms, and marital reconciliation sessions!

Oh Lord! But it would be okay now. Father Dan would have help. Finally. Miraculously. Because at a time when parishes were dying all over Cleveland, all across America, when parishes were being blended together in clusters, when there was a nearly decimating paucity of priests . . . when the Catholic Church, in some expert opinions, was dying except for Africa and South America and the Far East . . . it was truly *miraculous* that Father Dan, never mind the already doomed condition of the hair on his head, was finally granted an assistant by the big-shot diocesan mucky-mucks.

We saw our new priest for the first time at the ten o'clock Mass. He was assisting Father Dan. He was a big and powerful-looking man in his thirties. He *exuded* gravitas. His eyes were fierce in his belief in the Lord. His face was wide, set, and muscled. His expression was a glare and a glower.

And one more thing: He was black.

He was dark black. Black as coal. Black as the darkest, scariest night that parishioners in this nearly lily white congregation at Holy Angels could imagine.

"Father Africa," said Lukey, our youngest, and Lukey was dead-on: Our new priest, our Father Africa, was from the country of Uganda, in Africa.

Father Dan introduced Father Africa warmly, and our congregation gave Father Africa an equally warm round of applause. We weren't racists; the fact that one of the few black members of Holy Angels was a former Harlem Globetrotter basketball star was no accident; there just weren't very many black people living in Bainbridge Township.

Father Africa began to speak when we finished with our warm round of applause. I listened to him with the warmest expectation, hoping to be knocked out of my spiritual socks by his words. His voice was gloriously deep, the voice of God Himself. But he spoke with his face set mostly in a glare, flashing only a rare smile. Sometimes he avoided our eyes and stared down at the floor as he spoke. I had a lot of trouble understanding him.

"What did he say?" I whispered to Naomi. She shrugged.

I whispered the same question to my son Joe. He shrugged, too. So did Nick and John Law. I asked Lukey, too, but he thought I was goofing with him and pounded me as hard as he could, smiling winningly, on my arm.

Father Africa kept talking. I kept listening warmly. But I still couldn't understand more than a few words that he said. Oh well. At least I understood a *few* words. "Ja-eezus" sounded a bit like Deacon Fred's "Cheeze-us." And "Gud" was clear to me, as well as "Gud da Fada."

Father Africa finished his speech, went back to the altar, sat down with Father Dan, and stared at the floor as he prayed. I applauded Father Africa warmly, along with Naomi and our boys and everyone else sitting in church. As we were all applauding warmly and smiling, I glanced around and made eye contact with some of our church friends. A couple of them winked at me impassively; a couple of them raised their eyebrows at me; several of them shrugged. All of them looked as mystified as I was.

On the way out of church, I said to Naomi, "Do you have any idea what he said?"

She shot me an edgy look and whispered, "Of course I do. He spoke about Ja-eezus and Gud da Fada."

Father Dan and Father Africa were both standing in the vestibule as we walked out, waiting to shake hands with the congregation. Father Africa had a long line of people waiting to shake his hand warmly and to welcome him to Holy Angels Church. Father Africa stood there deadpan, his hand held out, hardly smiling.

Father Dan stood near him with hardly anyone there waiting to shake his hand. Father Dan had a rueful smile on his face that I interpreted as: "I may suddenly be chopped liver here, but it sure is nice to finally be getting some help."

I waited in line to shake Father Africa's hand, and when I got there and shook it, Father Africa smiled for a split second, then said something. Of course I couldn't understand it. I told him that I had a daughter who lived in Africa much of the year, but he looked at me blankly, like he didn't understand what I had said, either. Then he said something else, but I didn't understand that, either.

Then he shook my hand again and said, "Guh-bleh-hoo."

I walked away, mystified, and Naomi was waiting outside for me with the boys.

"How was he?" Naomi asked.

"Terrific."

"What did he say?"

"I have no idea."

"What do you mean you have no idea?"

"I didn't understand a word that he said."

Naomi said, "Maybe you need a hearing aid with all that rock and roll you abused yourself with. Like Bill Clinton."

"I don't need a hearing aid," I told her, "I didn't see that many Who concerts. He just has to stop speaking Swahili."

"I'm sure he doesn't speak Swahili," Naomi said archly.

"Guh-bleh-hoo."

"What?"

"*Guh-bleh-hoo.*"

"What does that mean?"

"I don't know. I don't speak Swahili."

"Oh, for God's sake," Naomi said.

I started to laugh.

"It probably means God bless you," she said.

"I didn't know you speak Swahili," I said.

"You're an idiot," Naomi said fondly.

I thought about it when we got home from church. Father Dan had told us in his welcoming speech that Father Africa would be with us for three years.

Three . . . *years*? Three years of Swahili?

"This is going to be a long three years," I said to Naomi.

"Maybe his English will get better."

"Couldn't the diocese have paid for some Berlitz courses for him before they made us his spiritual guinea pigs?"

"You're always complaining about the homilies anyway," Naomi said. "Is it better to understand a homily that isn't all that inspiring than it is to listen to a homily that you can't under-stand?"

I couldn't argue with that. That made perfect sense.

But as the weeks and months went by, something odd began happening to me when Father Africa said Mass. I was moved by him. Even though I still had little idea what he was saying dur-ing the homily, there was something physically moving about the way this big man said Mass.

His actions captivated me, transfixed me, as he mumbled the

prayers I couldn't understand. I glanced around and saw others in the congregation transfixed as well.

He did something during the Consecration that I had never seen and that I looked forward to seeing each time we went to a Mass that he said. He genuflected twice during the Consecration, and very softly he sang, "Ja-eezus we adore you, lay our lives before you, as we love you." As the weeks went by, he smiled more and more, too. His smile was joyous, childlike, and unexpectedly shy and vulnerable.

I realized I had come to like Father Africa very much, even though I could still barely understand him—but that didn't matter. He was conveying something to me without the necessity of words.

I liked him even more when, as I shook his hand after Mass, he said, "Wha-nem-gen?"

I said, "Joe."

He smiled. "Cho," he said. "Cho. Cho. Eas-a-remeba. Cho."

I smiled and said, "Yes, Father. Cho."

He said, "Guh-be-hoo, Cho."

I said, "*Guh-bleh-hoo,* too, Father. Thank you."

Now we understood each other.


MEL GIBSON WAS ARRESTED for drunk driving in California, down the Malibu street from where I had formerly lived, and in the course of his arrest fired off a barrage of anti-Semitic epithets at the arresting officer.

So that was it. Ball game. Open and shut. No doubt now. Mel was a raving anti-Semite. The man who had composed his prayer of a movie about Christ shared the mind-set of Adolf Hitler.

It made me want to retch. Mel had assassinated his own film.

Now the movie would be known for all time as a big-screen anti-Semitic billboard. It was said that in the course of making the film, Mel's own hands were used to drive the nails into Jesus's. And now, I thought, Mel had done it again—publicly and in full view of the world. He had driven his nail into his own movie.

He didn't even deny what he had said—at least not for long. It turned out there was a police videotape of the filth he had spewed. He went quickly away to some ideological rehab facility in rehab-rich Malibu.

*Man plans, God laughs.*

I still maintained that *The Passion of the Christ* was a prayer and not anti-Semitic filth, but then I was stubborn and I had certainly been wrong about a great many things in my life.

I KNEW MORE than a little about anti-Semitism personally. Not because I had studied and written about the Holocaust in Hungary for many years, but because I learned, when I was forty-five years old, that my father, who had been my lifelong hero and whose love had given me the confidence to become successful in life, had been a Nazi collaborator in wartime Hungary.

He hadn't been just a collaborator, he'd been part of the Hungarian Nazi government's Press Ministry. He'd organized book burnings and had cranked out the vilest anti-Semitic propaganda imaginable.

My father had kept this from me all of his life. He'd taught me that all men are equal. It was because of the things he had taught me as a boy that I became involved in the civil rights struggles of the 1960s. And it was no doubt because of the things he had taught me that I began studying the Holocaust in Hungary as a young man. It turned into a lifelong pursuit that caused me to take my now grown children to Dachau and Yad Vashem when they were little—so that *they* would never forget the meaning of the words *Never again.* When the Justice Department began deportation proceedings against my father in 1989, I learned the awful things he had done.

My heart was broken.

My relationship with my father, who was then eighty-two years old, was forever shattered. I decided then—in 1989—that he had lied to me my whole life and that everything he had taught me was hypocrisy . . . perhaps even designed to provide an alibi for himself someday. He could always say, if his past was revealed: "Who, me? But I have a son who is nationally known for his civil rights stands and for his writings about the Holocaust! So how can this possibly be true about me? If I was that kind of a man, would I have raised this kind of a son?"

I decided then—in 1989—that my father was a true-believing, heartfelt anti-Semite (like Mel Gibson), one of those sick Christian freaks who still blamed "the Jews" for crucifying Christ.

We barely had the semblance of a relationship after 1989. I didn't see my father for a long time. I hardly spoke to him on the phone. When I finally allowed him to visit his grandchildren, I scheduled meetings in Los Angeles for myself so that I hardly saw him during his visit.

My father kept saying two things to me over and over again: "Please forgive me" and "I've never lied to you"—which I considered the biggest whopper of them all.

He was in an old age home, dying at the age of ninety-four, when Naomi and I and our boys moved back to Ohio from California. I never saw him after we moved back. I knew he was dying and I didn't go to see him. I was dealing with my own recovery from throat cancer, but I was certainly well enough to see him. And I didn't.

His nurses called me from the old age home to tell me he was dying . . . and I still didn't go to see him. I let him die alone, knowing I was the only person in the world that he truly loved.

I told myself that I didn't go to see him because I had a trache in my throat and I didn't want my father, who loved me so much, to know that I had throat cancer. I told myself that I didn't go to see him because I didn't want to frighten and hurt him by letting him know that I had cancer. But as time passed after his death, I knew that was a lie, an excuse meant to shield my own heart against the hurt that I had done his. I had punished my father for what he had done by denying him my presence, my heart, and my hand at the moment of his death. He held some nurse's hand, I later heard, instead of mine. My father had given me a hand all of my life, but I wouldn't give him mine at the moment he needed it most.

As I began going to Holy Angels each Sunday, I felt an overwhelming, nearly paralyzing guilt about that. As Father Dan spoke of forgiveness and as I said the Our Father—"Forgive us our trespasses as we forgive those who trespass against us"—I couldn't shake the image of a frail ninety-four-year-old man holding a stranger's hand and saying, "Joe? Joe? Joe? Joe?" over and over again (a nurse informed me).

I had been told all of my life that I didn't hold grudges. I prided myself about not holding grudges in my professional and personal life. Through thirteen years of marriage, Naomi and I had never gone to bed still angry at each other over something at the end of the day. Naomi said that more than any other person she'd known, I wasn't at all afraid to say, "I'm sorry."

And now here I was, sitting in our pew at Holy Angels, listening to Father Dan talking about forgiveness as a cleansing of the heart and as a path to Christ . . . and I knew I still hadn't forgiven the person who'd helped and loved me the most. "Father, forgive them, for they know not what they do": He had forgiven them for the most inhuman tortures, for their savagery, for excruciating pain, for *crucifixion*! And I still couldn't forgive my own father, who had in an infinitely lesser way caused me infinitely less pain.

Part of my problem was that I was a writer, too, like my father, who had written in a different language in a different world. But I knew the power of the word more than most. And I wondered who had read my father's poisoned and poisonous words. (Jews were "parasites" who had to be "exterminated," and "the iron fist of the law" had to come down upon them.) And I wondered what those who had read my father's poisoned and poisonous words did to Jews after they had read them. Did those who read his words abuse and exterminate the Jews they found in their Hungarian neighborhoods? Did my father's words cause the injury or death of human beings? Because if they did, then my father was as guilty of murder as those who actually pulled the trigger or slit the throat. Was it possible, then, that the man I had loved so much and who had loved me so much was an accessory to murder? Or murders? Could I forgive that? Did Father Dan really expect me to forgive that?

I couldn't forgive him. As much as I tried, I couldn't forgive him.

But I began praying for my father on my walks and at night. The more I prayed for him, the more I seemed to remember our good times together: I'd learned the violin as a boy, and my father and I were playing our violins together, whooping joyously to some *csárdás;* or the time he'd gotten very angry at a clerk who'd cheated him and asked me in Hungarian how to say the eff word in English; or the time after my mother's death when he made a bean salad that had us running to the bathroom for a week.

I found myself, too, being not as judgmental about the things he had done in Hungary during the war. He lived in a completely anti-Semitic society. Was it possible that his anti-Semitism did not come from the heart, but was a poor, working-class kid's ploy to advance himself in his anti-Semitic world? Or a ploy to stay alive in a cruel and crazy Nazi world? Was that why there was not one single anti-Semitic word—*none*—in any of my father's thirty Hungarian-language novels? Because he really wasn't an anti-Semite, was he just pretending to be one?

(But, I rebuked myself, so what? Was that really any better? Was it less morally reprehensible to advocate the extermination of Jews for career reasons—to get ahead and make more money?)

And was it possible that he taught me not to be prejudiced—that only a person's character mattered, not creed or color—because he regretted what he'd done in Hungary? Was it an act of expiation on his part to raise a son who'd fight the forces of racism and anti-Semitism his whole life? Had he purposely constructed a bomb (his son) to blow up the tower of filth he'd created?

Was my father asking God to forgive him for what he had done by pointing to his son and saying: "Yes, Lord, I have done these things, but I have done this son, too, who stands for everything I wish I would have stood for"? Was my father making sure, since he loved me, that I wouldn't curse my own life as he had cursed his by doing the things he had done?

And wasn't I his greatest punishment? That the son he loved so much had turned against him, had frozen him from his heart, had left him alone at the moment of his death to hold the hand of a stranger who was being paid to be there? "Joe? Joe? Joe? Joe?" he had cried out over and over again in his final and ultimate plea for forgiveness. But Joe wasn't there; Joe was unforgiving, as cold as his father must have been when he wrote his injurious filth.

The day came, though, when Joe realized that he had cursed himself, too, by not being there to hold his father's hand. Joe felt that he needed to be forgiven, too, for abandoning his father. Joe knew in his heart that what he had done was cruel and heinous punishment for the cruel and heinous sins of his father.

It all clarified itself to me one afternoon as I was walking. If I was to be forgiven for what I had done to my father at his death, then I had to forgive him for what he had done in his life.

And so I did. I forgave him—grudgingly, almost against my will, to free myself of the leaden burden I had placed upon my-self, to blot the poison from my heart.

And so my father is dead, but he lives once again now inside my heart, just as alive as he ever was. We play the violin together again inside my heart, and we laugh. And in my imagination, we do something that we never did in real life.

We kneel together and we hold hands and we pray. We thank God for letting us understand, finally, our humanity. In my imagination, my father and I agree that we are each weak and sinful and need all the help God can give us.

I DECIDED that my Hollywood friend Loody was a holy man. A man my fictional Father Jack Turek would have been happy to call his pal.

Not because of his lifelong devotion to Our Lady of

she said, "I ain't gonna drink it—but you ain't got no call talkin' about beatin' nobody."

Loody smiled and said, "I ain't gonna beat you if you ain't gonna drink it. You just told me you ain't gonna drink it, so there ain't gonna be no beatin', okay?"

The woman said, "Okay." Then she smiled and said, "Thank you."

Loody smiled and said, "You're welcome," and walked away.

We ate dinner in Palm Springs that night, and Loody told the waiter, who was Hispanic, that we were going to do a movie about Our Lady of Guadalupe. He asked the waiter if he believed in Our Lady, and the waiter said he did.

When we left, the waiter followed us out and showed Loody a laminated holy card of Our Lady that was on his key ring along with photos of his three kids. The waiter kissed the holy card.

Loody dug into his pocket and gave the man everything he had, nearly two hundred dollars. The waiter was overwhelmed and didn't want to take the money.

Loody said, "Buy some toys for the kids. Nothing else, understand? No booze, no pills, no broads, no ponies, no Lotto. Just toys for the kids."

The man promised he'd buy nothing but toys for the kids.

"And thank Our Lady for it," Loody said.

The man nodded and kissed his Our Lady of Guadalupe holy card again. He said, "Yes, boss."

Loody said, "And don't call me 'boss.'"

The man smiled and said, "Okay, boss."

In the twin-turbo Mercedes, Loody asked to borrow five dollars from me. He didn't have any cash left. First thing the next morning, he returned the five bucks. He had cashed a check at our hotel. I didn't want to take the five dollars back. Loody said, "You got four kids to feed, you need the money."

Guadalupe or because he never missed Mass on Sundays. But because of his personal actions toward his fellow human beings. Loody was more Christ-like than some priests I had known.

Loody couldn't pass a homeless person without giving him or her all the money in his pocket.

He was driving his two-hundred-thousand-dollar twin-turbo Mercedes, a car he called "Blackie," one of only a thousand made in the whole world, when he saw a homeless black man sitting on a bench with his possessions.

"Look at him," Loody said, "he's given up."

Loody swerved wildly across two lanes of traffic to pull up to the man's bench. He reached into his pocket and pulled out all his cash and handed it to the man. It looked to me to be about fifty dollars.

"Don't drink it!" Loody said sternly to the man.

The man said, "I won't."

Loody said, "I mean it!"

The man said, "I know it," and we pulled away back into traffic.

In Palm Springs the next day, Loody passed a homeless woman on the street with a sign that said, "Need food."

Loody stopped, looked at her, reached into his pockets, and gave her all the cash he had. It was about a hundred dollars.

"Don't drink it," Loody said.

"Don't tell me what to do with it," the woman said. She already had the money in her hand.

"You want me to take it back?" Loody said.

"How you gonna get it back?" The woman smiled. "You gonna beat me?"

"Hell yes, I'm gonna beat you," Loody said, "I'll beat you into the damn ground."

The woman looked at him and smiled. "All right, all right,"

My friend Loody wasn't a saint. Nobody who knew him would ever call him that. There were no saints in Hollywood, only sinners who sinned on a grand, lavish scale. But you could still be a holy man in Hollywood, Loody proved, even if you weren't a saint, even if your sins were the feverish, lustful daydreams of ordinary men.

IT WAS SIX YEARS AFTER my throat surgery and I was here, in my surgeon's office, at the Cleveland Clinic, for my semiannual checkup.

It was a small white room. Naomi was sitting across from me. She was pale. On the way up here to the seventh floor, she was so nauseated that she stopped in the bathroom downstairs. She was nauseated before every one of my checkups through the years. In the car on the way here, as always, she said the rosary.

Marshall, my surgeon, the former head of ear, nose, and throat at the Harvard Medical School, perhaps the foremost throat surgeon in the world, was looking at the film of my throat that was taken by a tiny camera snaked through my nose a few minutes ago.

Marshall was staring at the screen, his brow wrinkled. He looked concerned. Naomi and I looked at each other. We were too afraid to look at the screen, so we kept our eyes on each other, supporting each other, holding each other with our eyes.

Marshall shook his head. He looked at me. "I can't believe this," he said.

I flinched. I closed my eyes in reflex. Was he about to tell me that he had seen something—a bump, a polyp, a protrusion, a growth? Darkened tissue?

Marshall said, "You're cured."

Naomi and I kept our eyes on each other. *What did he say? Did he really say that?* Did he really use that word? That word that's never used in oncology: *cured?*

*Cured?*

"I've never seen anything like this in more than thirty years of practice," Marshall said. "Your tissue is so regenerated you can't even tell there was ever a surgery, let alone a cancer here."

Naomi and I stared at him. We didn't know what to say. We sat there, our eyes still on each other, and then I saw tears forming in Naomi's eyes as she kept looking at me.

Marshall said, "This is really unbelievable. There's something else at work here, besides me." Marshall said, "This is a miracle."

Now we'd heard both of the never used, taboo magical words: *cured* and *miracle.*

"Your cancer's gone," Marshall said. "If you ever have cancer in your life again, it will have nothing to do with what happened in your throat."

Marshall said, "Congratulations."

Naomi and I still had our eyes on each other. We were both crying now. Marshall was staring at the screen again, shaking his head again, smiling.

I didn't know what to say. I felt like I'd been poleaxed or like I'd just smoked the most powerful joint in the world.

And then, suddenly, I knew exactly what to say.

I glanced upward, lifted my arms, and said, "Thank you, God."

I went over to Naomi, held her close, and whispered, "I love you."

We called my grown children and Naomi's brothers from the car on the way home and shared our joy with them.

We stopped on the way home at Holy Angels and sat in the chapel as the sun set, holding hands, not saying much.

Then we stopped off at Wal-Mart on this momentous day and bought all four of our boys a toy. When we got home, we hugged them, told them about our miracle, and gave them their toys.

And Lukey said, "Can we go to Dairy Queen after dinner and get an ice-cream cone?"

So we all had ice-cream cones after dinner at Dairy Queen.

It was the best ice-cream cone I'd ever had.

And before we fell asleep, the last thing Naomi said was, "Thank . . . you . . . Blessed . . . Virgin."

BUT . . . WHILE I CERTAINLY BELIEVED Marshall when he said that I was cured and thanked God for curing me . . . a part of me also knew it was very possible that I had just gotten a reprieve.

I had abused my body with tobacco and alcohol and sometimes other substances for most of my life. There would be a further price to pay, I was sure, *sometime*.

While my father had lived to be ninety-four, he had never smoked in his life and drank one Löwenbräu dark beer each Christmas Day. My mother, on the other hand, who chain-smoked and began most days with a shot of cognac (she drank nothing else alcoholic all day), died at the age of fifty.

I was afraid that in that sense I was a mama's boy.

I realized, though, that even if *someday* came tomorrow, I was at peace with it. Yes, of course I wanted to live—for Naomi and the boys and Steve and Suzi and Susie and the Cleveland Indians and the Rolling Stones and for a million other reasons. But if it ended tomorrow, I was at peace with it.

Because I believed in an afterlife now. I believed in the kingdom of heaven. I believed that God loved me. I believed that sinner though I was, I wasn't going to hell. I believed that I would see Him up there in His kingdom.

*Your will be done, not mine.*

I would thank Him for His cure and thank Him equally for His presence in my life . . . which I now knew wouldn't end with the end of my life.

While I wasn't convinced I was "cured," I was now unafraid of dying.

If I died, I would live in glory.

If I lived, I would live by His grace.

"YOU HAVE COMPLETED YOUR CANCER journey," said my friend Doug, the voice specialist at the Cleveland Clinic who'd seen thousands of cancer patients.

"I congratulate you for its outcome. Your journey, as it turned out, couldn't have been a happier one. Make sure that you understand what Marshall told you. *You are cured!* Make sure that you celebrate the moment, celebrate your cure, because a cure in cancer is so terribly rare. And remember those whose journey doesn't end this way. But celebrate and give thanks. You have been truly blessed."

On the way out of Doug's office, above his door, I saw a needlepoint that one of his students had given him. It was framed. It said, "With God all things are possible."

THE FEST was an annual Catholic celebration that attracted more than twenty thousand people to a field at a Cleveland seminary.

Held in the summer, it was a daylong event: Kids played games, gospel acts took to the stage, burgers and hot dogs and pierogis were consumed. It was a church picnic turned into a sacred rock-and-roll extravaganza, highlighted by the Mass that began as the sun went down and climaxed by a dazzling fireworks display.

It was Father Bob's annual show, a way to raise money for the seminary and the diocese. While admission to the Fest was free, raffle tickets for the cars being given away were a hundred dollars apiece.

And on the night of the Fest, with twenty-six thousand people in attendance, there I was, cross in hand, at the head of a procession of hundreds of priests and even a bishop. I was wearing a pink Tommy Bahama shirt, my Harley-Davidson jeans, my LeBron Nike sneakers, and a Rolling Stones hot-tongue silver ring.

Afterward, as fireworks exploded in the sky above us, Father Bob and I stood in the dark and we suddenly, joyously, hugged each other. We held glow sticks.

"Isn't this wonderful?" Father Bob said. "Isn't this amazing?"

And I yelled back, "It *is* amazing!" as the world exploded around us, as both of us grinned from ear to ear.

Father Bob said, "Thank you for being here."

And I said, "No, man, thank *you* for being here."

We were still grinning at each other when I suddenly realized that I was sky-high. Higher than a kite. Stoned silly. I'd often been stoned on booze in my life and on more substances than I cared to remember, but I'd never been this high before. Stone sober. High on God.

A banner above the altar/stage said, EXPECT A MIRACLE!— the theme of that year's Fest. But I had already gotten my miracle, and I was taking Doug's advice, celebrating it here in God's company.

I STILL GOT CHOKED UP when I talked about how I'd found God.

It was six years since I sat on that curb and sobbed and asked for His help.

I was with my best and oldest friends. Jerry and Gale were both attorneys. They were the smartest and most compassionate people I knew.

They were not particularly religious and they were Jewish. When I started wearing a cross around my neck six years ago, Jerry asked, "Why are you wearing that thing?"

Now, six years later, at my kitchen table during a barbecue, Jerry asked me: "How do you feel about religion now?"

I looked him in the eye and told him the truth: "Except for my family, my faith is the most important thing in my life. I feel God is in my heart. I feel a special glow that I can't even describe to you. It began that day I sat on the curb and asked God to help me, and it has been there every day of my life ever since. I know it's the presence of God. It has given me strength, serenity, and joy."

Jerry said, "What exactly happened that day you sat down on the curb and cried?"

And so I told Jerry and Gale about the most remarkable day of my life. My desperation that I couldn't win the fight against my addictions . . . the sweat pouring off of me . . . the mosquitoes and bugs trying to get into my trache . . . my knees shaking . . . the feeling that I couldn't breathe . . . my tears splattering off the concrete.

And suddenly I had to stop telling Jerry and Gale my story. I was choking up. There were tears in my eyes.

I continued: "I got up from the curb, and with His help, I walked. I took one step after another. And now, six years later, I'm still taking one step after another—with His help."

Jerry asked me how my faith had changed my life.

"I believe in prayer," I told him. "And I pray a lot. I pray at least an hour a day, maybe more. If I'm alone when I take my daily walk, I always pray. I have refocused my life completely on Naomi and the boys. They are my special blessings, and I thank God for them every moment of every day."

Jerry stared at me. He was very much a secular man, and I knew all this talk of God was too much for him.

Naomi suddenly said to him, "It's funny, though, it's not like Joe is a different person than he used to be. He's still as much fun as he was. The twisted little man who controls his writing is still there, but more muted or withdrawn or something. Joe's still bawdy, foul-mouthed, and joyously blue-collar, if you know what I mean."

Jerry grinned and said, "Well, I'm certainly happy to hear *that*."

We all laughed, and I said, "That twisted little man is still there, but he doesn't rule."

"Who rules?" Gale asked.

"God," I said, "and Naomi."

"I hope She and Naomi make you very happy," Gale said, smiling.

I said, "She and Naomi do."

When I walked Jerry and Gale back to their car later, Jerry said, "I'm glad we talked about you and God. You know I don't agree with everything you said, but I'm happy for you."

I hugged and kissed both of them and said, "I love you guys so much."

And I realized after I said it that I could never have said that before . . . before God graced me with His presence in my heart.

I had opened my heart on that curb six years ago and He had entered it.

I knew, too, what those tears were that choked me up every time I told the story of how I had found God.

They were tears of inestimable joy.

I WAS FULLY AWARE of the fact that as I spoke sometimes about my newfound faith—haltingly, shyly—some people looked at me like they were sure I'd gone gaga.

Many of those who looked at me with their eyeballs spinning, trying so hard to wipe the smirks off their faces, were old friends or associates who, like me, had always viewed the God-struck with derision or alarm. And now here I was, talking about God and Jesus in my life the same way the God-struck were talking about God and Jesus in their lives.

I understood why my friends' eyeballs were rolling. I knew what they were thinking. Maybe some alcoholic psychosis had belatedly showed itself. Maybe an undiagnosed paresis had savaged my brain. Or maybe my throat cancer had scared me so badly that I had conjured the image of Christ crucified . . . in the manner of those God-struck who claimed to espy the image of the Blessed Virgin Mary in paintings, home videos, cloud formations, crossword puzzles, car motors, seashells, and snowflakes.

I knew too that several of my old showbiz associates figured my new faith to be another in a long list of my opportunistic *moves*—another in an endless series of . . . *re-creations.*

They pointed out to the press that Joe Eszterhas was, after all, a Goldwater Republican (like Hillary, that other classic opportunist) in college. He then became a liberal lefty in the sixties (for the dope and the sex, probably). Which led him to that fountainhead of liberal lefty journalism, *Rolling Stone,* where he scored endless dope and endless sex. Which led him to a career in liberal lefty Hollywood, where he wrote liberal lefty movies (like *Betrayed* and *Music Box*). Which led him not only to primo dope and primo sex, but to primo *dollars,* too. Which led him to write liberal lefty bestselling books and more primo dollars.

Eszterhas then moved to Ohio for reasons that weren't clear but had something to do with either his cancer, his alcoholism, his divorce, his remarriage, his alimony payments, or the cataclysmic failure of *Showgirls* and *Jade* in the same year.

He moved to Ohio! To the Heartland! To the state that put George W. Bush over! . . . so, opportunist that he was, *of course he found God.* In Ohio. In the Heartland. He hadn't found God in Mill Valley or San Rafael or Tiburon or Lahaina or Malibu.

No, he suddenly found God *after he moved to Ohio.*

Hadn't Paul Verhoeven, the director of *Basic Instinct,* once said that Eszterhas had taken the side of gay protesters against the movie that he'd written, his own movie, because of his opportunism? Because Eszterhas was afraid, according to Verhoeven, of fanatical homosexual storm troopers who'd invade his hilltop Tiburon home and play *Clockwork Orange* with his wife and children? And hadn't Michael Douglas, the star of *Basic Instinct,* flat-out called Eszterhas "a Machiavellian opportunist"?

The truth was that I was self-conscious speaking about my faith, about God and Jesus, because I knew how cockeyed "all this God stuff"—as one of my friends put it—sounded coming from me. It not only went against my lifelong public image, it torched it. No, it *immolated* and nuked it.

I was the bad boy. The wild hair. The rogue elephant. The drinking, drugging, effing wild man. The man who tore a *swath* through Vegas while "researching" *Showgirls.* The cocaine cowboy. The weed eater. The tequila king. The Hollywood animal proud that he was a Hollywood animal.

And now I was holding on to a cross at the ten o'clock Mass at Holy Angels Church and raising it high for the world to see. And now I was praying every day and loving my wife and raising my children. Quietly. Out of the public eye. No booze, no bimbos, no coke, no weed, no tequila, no "research."

I wasn't raising hell anymore.

I was raising a cross instead of raising hell.

"You behaving yourself?" a Bainbridge Township cop asked me when I ran into him on my walks. I grinned and said, "Yes," and he grinned and said, "I almost can't believe it." He told me he'd followed my career for decades. "I almost can't believe it, either," I said to him, and we both laughed.

There were moments when I almost rolled my eyes at myself as I thought about "all this God stuff." How in the eff could I have done this to myself? Maybe it *was* paresis or alcoholic psychosis or terminal nicotine withdrawal. But I knew, thinking about "all this God stuff," that that wasn't true.

Because I was happy.

I was happier than I'd ever been in my life.

It was like I had always had a hole in my heart that was finally filled.

There was a joy in my heart that had never been there, a joy that contained an inner peace I had never known but had self-destructively always been seeking.

It was God's grace. God had blessed me (undeservedly). God loved me (undeservedly). God had granted me His (or Her) grace.

I had become God-struck.

And yet, knowing all that, I felt the need to insist that I hadn't lost my mind when I was asked publicly about my faith. I said, "Just because I have a newfound and deep belief in God doesn't mean I've somehow been lobotomized or anything." And once I even said, "Believing in God doesn't mean I've been lobotomized or castrated, either, you know."

I read somewhere that Great Britain's former prime minister, Tony Blair, said that he was reluctant, too, to talk about his faith. "You talk about your faith publicly and people think you're a nutter," said Blair.

I liked that a lot. I've viewed Tony Blair ever since as my fellow "nutter." One of his aides said that Blair "doesn't fit the image of a typical pious person because he's pretty irreverent, he swears a fair bit and . . . if he sees a very attractive woman, his eye will wander and all that stuff."

*Effing ay, Tony! Right on, boyo!* Although (I don't care what Naomi says) my eyes don't wander and I never look at other attractive women at Holy Angels Church. I only look at Naomi.

Blessed be the name of the Lord!

Blessed be the name of Naomi!

I HAD MY MOMENTS OF DOUBT and pain still—even after my journey of faith. I asked God to forgive me for these moments when I doubted His existence, but then I decided there was nothing He had to forgive me for.

I believed in Him, but I was human. And for almost all of my life, except for the recent past, I had been very cynically human . . . or very humanly cynical.

And now here I was, walking around talking about having God in my heart and feeling like I'd never felt before. Carrying on about peace and love and serenity and choosing daylight instead of darkness.

Yet in my moments of doubt and pain, I said to myself: Are you sure about *all this stuff, son? All this stuff* that you have always rejected, scoffed at, laughed at, and made fun of?

You watched your mother babbling crazily, feverishly, as she died, waving these worn black beads about with her scrawny arms. And after she died, you walked out of that foul, stink-filled room and smoked a cigarette outside and slugged down half a glass of Scotch whiskey and thought to yourself: That poor, deluded woman, babbling incoherently, her eyes burning, saying the name "Jesus" over and over again. . . . That poor, uneducated, simple-minded, innocent, crazed, ravaged, war-torn, violated skin and bones of a woman . . . swallowing all that pious, saintly, sweet-scented bullshit right to the very end . . . till her final gasp of air and claw of my palm. . . . That poor, deluded shell of a human being beaten bloody by her life, beaten to death finally by the metastasizing monster born again and again in different places inside her, more tumor than flesh and blood at the very end . . . and she swallowed all that sanctimonious, holy, hokey crap and finally died.

*Eff God!* That's what I thought when I was twenty-three years old. *All that stuff* really was the opiate of the masses. What the eff could my poor mother, who had nothing else, hold on to . . . except God (and her son) at the end? Because thanks to the God that she loved so much, she *had* nothing else.

She had lost her country and was living in a foreign place that she feared. She had lost her language and could communicate only with those Hungarians who lived in her strudel ghetto or went to her church. Her marriage had died someplace in the barracked misery of the refugee camps or in the squalor of the maggoted apartment she lived in with her unfaithful husband and her untrustworthy son. Her son was part of that America she feared and he was speaking as much English as Hungarian. She was humiliatingly poor. The only piece of jewelry she owned was her wedding band. She owned no clothes but the glad rags she picked from bins during rummage sales at the Volunteers of America or the Salvation Army.

She didn't even have her own mind anymore. She had lost that, too. Aliens from outer space came through the door locks and the electric plugs of her schizophrenia and had stolen her mind. And since she didn't have her mind anymore, she didn't have any friends, either.

My mother was that poor crazy woman mumbling to herself, dressed in rags, shuffling up and down Lorain Avenue on Cleveland's West Side to the market and to her church and back, chain-smoking the American cigarettes she loved so much as she went back and forth.

No, she had nothing else except God and Jesus and the Blessed Virgin Mary (and my hand and my heart) right to the end. And I had walked out of that wretched, nightmarish room with the oxygen tents everywhere and said, Eff all this! . . . and lit up a cigarette and swilled some Scotch and said: All this stuff, this Jesus bullshit, this mindless pious Holy nonsense: It will never be for me.

Forty years later, it *was* for me: everything I had ridiculed, scoffed at, and laughed at and made fun of. *All that stuff* was a part of the deepest part of my life. The cigarettes and the booze were gone along with my crazy, loving, schizophrenic mom, and there were many days now when I, my mother's son, fell asleep praying, the last word on my lips before I fell asleep the name of Jesus.

I believed in God deeply, but I had my moments of doubt and pain when I knew that I had sucked on the opium just like my mother and it had had the same effect on me. I especially had moments of doubt and pain when something terrible or heinous happened to someone very young, very innocent, or very good. That seemed to happen often, so my moments of doubt and pain came often, too.

At one of those moments I suddenly remembered the fervor in my mother's eyes when she prayed. This woman who had never had much and who had lost everything that she did have . . . never complained or asked anything from God. All she did in her prayers was fervently thank Him. That's all she did. *Thank* God. And in her most awful, heartbreaking moment of pain, at her death, gasping for air and clawing my hand, I never saw a flicker of doubt on her face. She kept thanking God with every gasp that she had left. And then she died her brutal, grotesque death. And I left the room and said, Eff all this, and smoked my cigarette and drank my Scotch.

But now I remembered her eyes in my moments of doubt and pain. And I remembered her thanking God for everything. And now I thanked God for allowing me to see my mother in those horrible final intimate moments. And I thanked my mother for sharing her agony and belief and courage with me.

My memory of my mother's eyes at those moments, I knew, would allow me to keep my faith, my belief in Him, during my future moments of doubt and pain.

WE MISSED HOLY ANGELS CHURCH badly when we drove on our annual Clark Griswold Family Vacations to Florida: to Amelia Island or Longboat Key or Disney World.

We always went to church on Sundays wherever we were, but we felt displaced and disoriented.

I was envious of those who were carrying the cross in these strange churches and noticed that almost all of the crossbearers were kids: Was I going to be replaced at Holy Angels one day soon by . . . my sons? (I looked forward to that.)

The priests in these resort/retirement community churches tended to be older. Many of them, I discovered, were former army, navy, or marine chaplains who still said Mass at different bases nearby.

We were hypnotized by an old Spanish church in Fernandina Beach. It was a dark and gloomy place of ghosts and shadows, a world away from the bright airiness of Holy Angels.

The music in almost all of the strange churches we were visiting was old-style hymnal. I missed Christie, who wrote many of her own songs at Holy Angels and charmed us with their melodies and insights.

After visiting a lot of strange churches, I even missed Father Dan's homilies. ("But I thought you liked my homilies," Father Dan will say after reading this book, and I will say: "I do . . . like . . . *some* of them.") And Father Dan will say, "Well, you certainly quote a *lot* of them."

Not only did I miss Father Dan's homilies, but—I swear to God—I even missed Deacon Fred in all his blessed glory.

I even missed Jesus's name not pronounced "Cheeze-us!"

We finally figured out a way of softening the pain of not being able to go to Mass at Holy Angels when we were on vacation. We took the CDs of Christie's choir with us on our trips. We played them in the car on the way to our strange churches and then on the way back to the beach.

Once, on a particularly glorious afternoon on Amelia Island, with the boys romping joyfully in the surf on their boogie boards, Naomi and I played our Holy Angels CD.

We sat there in our beach chairs, holding hands, watching our boys, listening to Christie's songs. We were blissfully happy and home at Holy Angels. It was a moment of prayer out there on the sand. No words were necessary.

I KNEW THAT my daughter Suzi had contempt for God, so I was nervous and afraid when I told her that I'd been saved. She was almost thirty years old and had always scoffed, like her father, at those who claimed to have found God.

Suzi and I had been the closest of friends until I divorced her mother when Suzi was seventeen years old. I had shared and encouraged Suzi's love of wildlife and then of photography. We went on countless zoo visits and whale-watching adventures together. Suzi came to *me,* not her mother, with news of her first period. "No one will ever love you as much as I do," I Magic Markered in big letters on the wall of her room in the house we had lived in in Tiburon.

But the divorce came close to destroying our relationship, partly because Suzi was headstrong, passionate, and stubborn— like her father. She hated me for leaving her mother, as she hated Naomi and her little half-brothers. Oh, she went through the niceties sometimes—barely—but she didn't argue with me when

I said, "You're a hater, Mo"—my nickname for her—"that's what you are."

Our postdivorce visits were strained. Eight years had gone by since the divorce when I was diagnosed with throat cancer, and though Suzi was there from California during most of my hospitalization, it was painfully obvious that she could barely stand being in the same room with Naomi.

There was, too, another reason for the distance between us. She had been living for several years now with Adam, a young man I loathed. If she had difficulty hiding her hatred of Naomi, then I had the same difficulty hiding my loathing of Adam. I considered Adam a parasite. He lived off the money that Suzi gave him, the money that her parents gave *her*—which meant that Adam lived off of *me,* since my ex-wife's money came from *my* earnings and the divorce settlement.

Adam was the kind of jobless phony who would order the most expensive item on the dinner menu, then get back to the home that Naomi and I and the boys shared in Malibu and say, "Do you have any good port?"

He was an allegedly reformed junkie who had no idea what he was going to do with his life. One week he was going to be a poet, the next a chef, the next a real estate developer. He borrowed Suzi's car one Fourth of July weekend to pick up a friend at the airport and disappeared (leaving Suzi carless) for three days. Her brother Steve's friends told him that they knew Adam cheated on Suzi—even taking other women to the house where he and Suzi lived when Suzi was out of town visiting me.

On the occasions when Suzi and Adam visited us together, Adam sneakily tried to flirt with Naomi—who thought him such a creep that she refused to sit in the backseat of the car with him while Suzi sat up front talking to me.

I spoke with Steve about all this, and while he shared my feelings about Adam, he warned me not to say anything to Suzi. "You know how she is, Pops," Steve said. "It'll just hurt your relationship with her even further."

Still, I couldn't stop myself sometimes and mildly expressed my concerns about him. "He'll be the perfect husband for me," Suzi replied. "He's not at all an alpha male like you, Dad. I can go off and do my nature photography around the world, and he can stay home, clean the house, walk the dog, arrange my photography files, and take care of the baby. Adam is perfect for all that."

"Is that really the kind of husband you want?" I asked her.

And when she said yes and laughed, I said, "Well, why don't you just hire a good-looking assistant instead?"

"Don't, Dad!" she said, and the anger I suddenly saw flash in her eyes made me back off.

I saw that same look in her eyes when, during a visit shortly after my surgery, I told her about my new relationship with God. She said coldly, "Great, good for you, Dad." Her eyes said, "Do you really expect me to believe this shit? To take it seriously? After everything you've said in the past about God and the people who believe in God? Maybe you're going through some kind of chemical imbalance or pre-senility, but don't talk to *me* about it."

I saw something else in her eyes when I spoke to her about God. Pity. She looked at me like I had become some kind of drooling fool, ready to be wheeled from my stupid church to a nice smiley face neighborhood nursing home. The look on Suzi's face warned me that she was ready to begin wheeling.

She came to visit us with Adam again a few months later. Adam and I almost got into it when I said we were going to have lunch in the West Side neighborhood where I'd grown up and Adam said, "We're going to have lunch in the ghetto, huh?"

And I said, "I didn't grow up in the ghetto, Adam." Adam looked away and grinned.

His backseat hanky-panky with Naomi (he always managed somehow to "accidentally" bump into her) was so out of hand that I had to forcefully tell Suzi to sit in the back with Adam, even if the backseat made her carsick.

My relationship with Suzi reached the breaking point because of that visit. I'd had enough. I didn't want that creep—who'd insulted both my wife and my daughter *and* me with his actions—in my house again. So when Suzi called from California to say they were coming to visit us at Thanksgiving, I told her I'd love to see her but not Adam. Adam couldn't come. Adam couldn't ever step inside my house anymore. Period. End of discussion.

Suzi, as Steve had forecast, went nuclear. "You're not going to let the man I'm going to marry, the future father of my children, into your house?"

I said, "You're not going to marry him. You'll come to your senses sometime. And as far as having children is concerned, I hope you're having protected sex."

Then she went thermonuclear: "It's none of your effing business what kind of sex we're having! If Adam can't come, then I'm not effing coming, either! And as long as Adam can't come, that's how long I'm not coming! If you don't want to see him, then you're not going to see me, either!"

"Listen, Mo," I said, "you know how much I want to see you. I love you."

She was crying now. She said, "No, you don't."

"You *know* how much."

She said, "No. If you loved me, you wouldn't be doing this. I know you don't like Adam. You've never liked Adam. You hate Adam."

"I don't," I said. "I don't hate him."

"Yes, you do," she said. "You hate him the same way I hate Naomi. But I *swallow* my hatred of her. For *you,* Dad! I don't say, 'I'll see *you,* but not with *her* around.' I could say that, but I don't. Because of *you,* Dad! Because I love *you* so much. But you don't love *me* that much because that's what *you're* saying. You'll see me but without him. That's not fair. Not after what I've had to do—not after I've swallowed my feelings because of you."

It was out in the open now, so I told her, finally, honestly, how I felt about Adam and why. How I felt he was using her on a variety of levels. The only thing I didn't tell her was that he was cheating on her and that he wouldn't stop flirting with my wife. I didn't tell my daughter those things because our crisis was already excruciatingly painful. I didn't want to lay that kind of hurt on her.

Our talk ended with Suzi saying, "I don't know you anymore, Dad. I've never understood why you moved back there. I don't understand why you like all those hicks back there so much. You're not the Dad I knew. You and all your crap about God and church. *What's wrong with you?* The only people who ever go to church are losers. That's what you used to tell me. Look at you now, with all those dumb crosses you've got everywhere. You live in some kind of holy Halloween house, you know that, Dad?"

She hung up, crying. I told Steve about our blowup and he said, "I told you, Pops. You should have left it alone."

I said, "I couldn't do that anymore. She's talking about marrying Adam and having kids with him. I just can't stand by and do nothing when I'm convinced she'd be making the biggest mistake of her life. I'm her dad. It's part of my parental responsibility. I'd tell *you* if I thought you were effing up *your* life."

"I know," Steve said, "but you know how Suzi is."

She sent me a nasty letter. I sent her a nasty one back. We knew we were both violating a basic rule we had always agreed upon: Don't put your anger into writing. She sent me another nasty letter saying she wouldn't see me as long as I wouldn't allow Adam into my house. I sent her a letter saying she shouldn't for her own good issue this ultimatum to me. I was a cancer patient in remission; I wasn't a young man anymore. We didn't know how much more time we'd have in our relationship. I told her I didn't want her forever haunted by her refusal to see me.

There were no more letters and no more calls. I prayed for her every morning and every night, but I was reduced to asking Steve how she was and what she was doing. She was fine, Steve always said, off to Australia or Africa to shoot wildlife. I heard she spent thirteen hours sitting in a jeep once at the Serengeti waiting for a lion to come by. She was apprenticing with the BBC. She and Adam had bought a dog.

And then one day Steve told me that she and Adam had broken up. The answer to my prayers, I thought. Thanks be to God, the creep was out of her life! Maybe, I thought, I'd hear from my Mo now. Maybe she'd call and say, "You were right, Dad! He was a creep. I can't believe I didn't see it sooner. I miss you! I love you! When can I come out to see you?" And I'd say, "Now! Get on a plane right now! You won't ever believe how much I missed you! Remember what I wrote on your wall: 'No one will ever love you as much as I do.' Come now! I'll pay for your flight. I'll pick you up at the airport!"

But I got no call. Weeks passed. Months passed. A year passed. Then two. Then three.

I prayed daily for her health and safety. I woke up once in the middle of the night, badly startled, thinking I'd heard her voice saying: "Dad?" *Dad? Dad? Dad? Dad?* I carried in my pocket the little Eskimo sculpture she had given me many years ago for Christmas.

On each of my birthdays, as I got older, she sent me nothing, not even a card. On my sixtieth birthday, after a wonderful day with Naomi and the boys, I fell asleep trying not to cry. I had been waiting all day for a phone call from Suzi, just a short call saying, "Happy birthday, Dad."

You are only sixty once in your life; living sixty years is a significant event. But there was no call from Suzi. No, Steve told me on my sixtieth birthday, Suzi wasn't in any exotic location (Africa, Bali) where it may have been hard to get to a phone. Suzi was in Tiburon with my ex-wife.

Another year went by, and one day, I thought I heard God say, "Why don't you call her?"

*Me?* Call *her?* I was her father. And I was a cancer patient. And she hadn't even called me on my sixtieth birthday. And now *I* was supposed to . . . *call her?*

I told Steve I was thinking about calling her. He told me not to do it. "I don't want you getting more hurt, Pops," he said.

I swallowed my pride. I kept thinking I heard God's voice telling me to call her. I wasn't about to say no to God. So I called her one summer afternoon after I came in from my walk. I said a prayer and then dialed her cell phone number.

She picked up, said hello, and I said, "Hi, Suzi."

And she said, "Dad?" She sounded excited hearing my voice.

I said, "It's nice to hear your voice, Mo."

She said, "It's nice to hear yours, too."

We both laughed self-consciously at the same time. I heard a car horn in the background. She said she was racing to an appointment and was caught in heavy traffic. "Dad," she said, "I hate to ask you this, but I'm really late for this appointment. Can you call me tomorrow at the same time?"

I said, "Sure. Bet on it. I'll call you at the same time. Will you be there?"

"I'll be here." She laughed.

I said, "I love you."

She said, "I love you, too."

I hung up. I was smiling. She *had* sounded excited, and it had felt *so* good to hear her voice. I thanked God for letting me hear *His*.

I was so jubilant that night that I celebrated by having two extra glasses of cranberry juice. I called Steve to tell him that she'd been excited to hear from me, and he said, "Well, wait till you really talk to her, Pops. You haven't really talked to her yet."

I wasn't worried. I had heard the sound of my daughter's voice and it was the old Suzi, my Mo who loved me.

I was sky-high when I called her the next day. But her voice was instantly flat and cold. I was suddenly frightened. I tried to make small talk. I spoke about the weather and asked about the traffic in the Bay Area because it sounded to me like she was in a car again. She was saying nothing, just letting me prattle on like an old fool.

And then she said, in a voice so icy and dead that I wouldn't have recognized it: "You think you're going to chitchat with me, Dad? Is that what you think you're going to do?"

I said, "What's the point in going over our differences—there's no point, is there? Let's just go on—"

She said, *"Oh yes, there is!"* Her voice was angry now. "You're going to have to apologize to me, Dad!"

I said, "Maybe we should both apologize and try to move on."

*"Oh no!"* she said. "No, Dad! You're not going to get away with this! You apologize for all the hateful things you said about Adam. For the awful things you wrote to me in your letters." She was yelling at me now.

"You left *me*," Suzi yelled, "when you left Mom!"

"No, I didn't," I said. "I love you—"

*"No, you don't!"* She was screaming at me now. "Eff you, Dad! Eff you!"

Maybe I was too old for it. Maybe the past six years had beaten me up too much. Maybe I just had to stop myself from getting hurt anymore. I hung up. I sat there, my heart broken. I felt like I was going to throw up.

Naomi came in and put her arm around me and held me.

I knew now that I had lost my daughter.

My daughter was gone from me.

I asked God to forgive me.

As time passed, Steve kept me up-to-date. She was in Alaska again. She was in Africa again. She had a cover photo in a national magazine.

I saw her at Steve's wedding a couple of years after we had spoken on the phone. She looked beautiful. We hugged each other clumsily when we first saw each other. Then we avoided each other for the next two days. We never spoke, although I did see her glance at the little silver cross I wore around my neck.

*No one will ever love you as much as I do, Mo.*

IN 1967, when I was twenty-three years old, Pam, a girlfriend I'd recently broken up with, told me she was pregnant. Blood tests determined there was very little doubt that I was the father. Pam decided to have the baby and put it up for adoption through Catholic Charities.

The baby, a girl, was born in April of 1968 and put up for adoption. A girlfriend of Pam's sent me a baby picture with this scrawled on the back: "She looks like your mother, I hear." Pam and I went separate ways. She married, had a child, got divorced, then married again. I got married and had two children with Gerri—our son, Steve, and our daughter, Suzanne Maria.

I had no contact with Pam through the years, but I never forgot that I had another daughter out there somewhere. I almost started to search for her. But a close friend who was an attorney stopped me. He himself had an adopted son, and he felt very strongly that if the biological father showed up at his door, it would be unfair to him. "If she wants to," my friend told me, "she'll find you."

In 1996, shortly after my divorce and remarriage, I got a message through the Writers Guild of America that a young woman was trying to reach me "on a very personal matter." I knew in my heart instantly who it was. I had an assistant call the young woman to tell her to write me a letter. I got it within days.

The letter was smart, witty, funny. She was my daughter, she wrote, and she'd tracked me down through Catholic Charities. She was twenty-nine years old, a publishing executive in Phoenix—a writer, like me. No children, divorced. She wanted nothing from me, she wrote, except to meet me and ask me some medical questions and questions about my family history. Her name jarred me—it was Suzanne Maria Warner. The coincidence was flabbergasting. How could she possibly have the same name as my other daughter—Suzanne Maria Eszterhas?

I invited her to my home in Malibu. As she came through the big gates and I watched her from the den, the hairs on the back of my neck stood up. She looked exactly like my mother, whom I had loved so much, who had died holding on to my hand thirty years ago. She didn't resemble my mother—she *looked exactly like her.*

Susie stayed at my house for two days, and we talked. She had been telling the truth in her letter, I saw. Her visit was an interview. She wanted to know about genetic things, about family history. Our meeting wasn't really successful. We were off balance and clumsy with each other. There was no real warmth between us. She seemed totally wrapped up in her work—she was the compleat corporate executive. I supposed that I must have seemed wrapped up in my work to her, too. I had a new movie opening. I was doing interviews every day. It was very possible that I seemed full of myself to her, too.

She visited again some months later with Bruce, the man she was dating. He was in the T-shirt embroidery business. It was the same as before, maybe even worse. I'd invited Steve and Suzi Eszterhas to meet Susie Warner, and they didn't seem to like her much. They actually seemed to like Bruce, who was seventeen years older than Susie, more.

I felt no spark with my newfound daughter, although we resolved the coincidence of her name matching Suzanne Maria Eszterhas's. The nuns at the adoption agency had named her, Susie said, for Pam's mother (Susan) and mine (Maria). Gerri and I had named Suzi Eszterhas for Gerri's mother (Susan) and mine. (The "Suzanne" in both cases probably came from the worldwide popularity of Leonard Cohen's song.) It was a bizarre coincidence. Both babies had been named after different grandmothers who had the same first name.

As I said good-bye to Susie Warner after her visit, I wasn't sure I'd ever see her again—she didn't seem like she'd had much fun with me. She seemed in a hurry to leave.

I didn't hear from her for almost four years. She didn't call me and I didn't call her. She finally called after the media reported that I had throat cancer, during the period when I could barely talk.

She was sorry I was so sick, she said. She had thought often of calling me but wasn't sure that I wanted to talk to her again.

She was praying for me. Her life had changed. She had married Bruce and was now Suzanne Maria Perryman. She had quit her executive job at the publishing company. She had two little girls, Zoe and Olivia—my first grandchildren. She was going to church each Sunday, and God had a very special place in her life.

We started talking on the telephone a lot. I told her how my life had changed. I told her about trying to deal with my two addictions and with my cancer and how difficult I was finding that. I told her how I had found God on that blistering day and asked her to pray for me. We talked about God a lot. Susie understood exactly what I meant when I said I felt God in my heart because she had God in her heart, too. She sent me holy cards she had saved from her childhood. I felt closer and closer to her. She was my friend, the daughter I had abandoned almost forty years ago, the daughter who had given me my first grandchildren, the daughter whose belief in God was a staff to lean on during my time of trouble.

One day she asked me for advice. She said she thought something was wrong with Zoe, her youngest daughter, who was two years old. Susie didn't think Zoe was developing normally. Others—including Zoe's local doctors—disagreed with her and told her to leave it alone, but Susie couldn't. She was concerned that Zoe had some kind of undiagnosed developmental disease. I told her to trust her own maternal instincts and forget everything everyone else was telling her. I knew a lot of people at the Cleveland Clinic. Let's see what the Clinic knew about this kind of stuff, I said to Susie.

I called her back days later to report that the Cleveland Clinic was one of the best places in the world for the developmentally disabled. Susie had been doing some research, too, and she said her research told her the same thing. I arranged an appointment for Zoe through the people I knew at the Clinic.

I was moved profoundly the first time I held Zoe. She had my deep brown eyes and my big, round head. I thought she was the sweetest little girl in the world. Naomi and I went with Susie and Zoe to their appointments at the Clinic.

By the end of the first day, we were reeling. Zoe had a genetic metabolic illness called mitrochondrial disease. A part of her brain was missing. The disease was degenerative and progressive, and there was no cure. It would only get worse. Zoe could even go blind.

Many people who had this disease died in their twenties. It was a rare disease, a genetic freak. *Both* parents had to have the gene that caused the disease. If Susie had married anyone other than Bruce, her daughter wouldn't have been sick. If Bruce had married anyone other than Susie, his daughter wouldn't have been sick.

What a sadness. What an overwhelming sadness. We were riven. Susie was devastated, but I admired her strength so much. Chip off the old block, I bragged to myself. She kept her chin up. She carried on. Only when I accidentally opened her bedroom door thinking she wasn't there did I see her crying. She was lying on the bed in the dark room, Zoe asleep next to her. Susie was lying very still, her eyes closed, praying, the tears running silently down her face.

Sometime later she discovered that Olivia had the same disease. I was decimated for Susie, even though I knew that she wouldn't allow herself to be decimated.

Ollie had this same hellish degenerative disease! For which there was no cure. Which would only get worse with the passing of time. I thought of something Susie had written to Zoe:

*I will always love you. You are my daughter and I will never stop. I will never stop looking for doctors who do not roll their eyes at the complex biochemical patterns that define your disease. I will never stop looking for more ways to improve your health—and better methods to manage your disease. These are my lifelong promises to you.*

Now the same promises Susie had made to Zoe applied to Ollie as well.

*It was decimating.* It was tragic.

One day on the phone as she ended her conversation, she said, "Good night. I love you." She hung up.

I sat there for a few moments, tears in my eyes, and I called her back. "I love you, too," I said.

It was the first time we'd said it to each other.

She wrote an essay that she sent me about the day we heard Zoe's diagnosis:

*And then the time came when I needed my father and he was there— understanding my desperate need to find a diagnosis for my sick little girl, and he too became her advocate, connecting me with the right doctor—the one who could finally tell us what was wrong and how our life would be. He sat with me, sharing my hurt, touching me briefly as we tried to understand the words the doctor spoke. We went on a drive later that day, my father, his wife, and I. We traveled up and down winding streets and I watched the newly bright green trees against the radiant blue of the afternoon spring sky. The scenes slipped by my backseat window while I sat struggling with the silence. Searching for the right words to thank him for being there, words that could reflect the rawness of my emotion. I looked up and saw my father's deep brown eyes, holding me, framed in the rearview mirror. Meeting his gaze, I watched his eyes darken with emotion. I understood then that I had finally found sameness. They were my very own eyes, looking back at me.*

Susie brings both girls to the Cleveland Clinic now. The news is never good, but on lucky days it's not *all* bad. There is no hope for a medical reversal, though Susie never gives up. Her days are filled with doctor's appointments and lab tests. Zoe has begun losing her eyesight now, and Susie spends her days making sure that Zoe sees as much of life as she can—*a flower! a butterfly! the lions at the zoo!*

She does her best, too, to deal with Zoe's tears. "You cry many different tears," Susie wrote her daughter. "Raindrop tears that trickle down your cheeks like gentle rain runs against a window. Thunderstorm tears that are fast and furious, and the torrential downpour which falls hard and steady and seems to be endless."

Susie and I know that it is our shared pain that has brought us so close together. We are truly father and daughter now, fighting together for her daughters, for my grandchildren. We are friends.

I can't help thinking of my mother each time I look at her. Like my mother, Susie won't have an easy life. Zoe and Ollie will cry more and more each year. But like my mother, Susie has God at her side. And me. And Bruce.

I pray often during the course of a day for Zoe and Ollie. And I thank God for my greatest gift. For giving back to me the daughter I abandoned. His gift revealed a divine generosity that I knew I didn't deserve.

*I need two more miracles, my Great Friend. Two more miracles for two dazzling little girls. And for the daughter I abandoned, who teaches me something about bravery and responsibility every day.*

We are all crossbearers. We are all weak, but we do our best to carry our crosses.

We must help one another with our crosses. Because every time we help someone with a cross, we help Him with His.

She says: "I do. All the time."

Good, Estelle, pray more. I will pray for you, too.

Oh, and *Estelle,* one more thing. You have to stop smoking.

She says, "I have—finally."

Good, then have hope, Estelle. You can live, Estelle. You can live. Have hope. You must have hope!

She says, "I try."

I held her hand and I said a prayer with her. I told her to call me if she needed help of any kind. She smiled and said, "Oh no, I wouldn't impose."

I said, "You won't be imposing." I said, "You're going to need all the help you can get."

She said, "I know."

She had tears in her eyes. So did I. I held her. I hardly knew her, but I had difficulty letting her go. I took the yellow wristband that said LIVE STRONG from my arm and I gave it to her. She took it. She put it on her arm. Her hands shook.

I heard nothing from her for months. Then a woman came to see me as I sat in church. She said she was Estelle's friend. Estelle was not well, she said. She'd had surgery and had to have chemo and radiation, too. She'd almost died from the radiation. Her tumor had shrunk, but then it grew back. She was in Phoenix now, at a place where they used experimental drugs.

Four or five months later, I am at a service station pumping gas when I see someone smiling at me from the passenger side of a pickup truck. It is a face shrunken and wraithlike.

I go to her. Estelle smiles. She tries to say something, but she can't speak. All that's left to hear of her voice is her breath.

A young woman gets into the driver's seat of the pickup. She introduces herself. She is Estelle's daughter.

I introduce myself. I am Estelle's friend.

———

ESTELLE, LIKE ME, was in her mid-sixties. She wore a layer of scarves on this hot day. She said hello to me in the church parking lot after Mass. Her voice was as raspy and weak as mine. I knew what she was going to say before she said it. I had seen the lump underneath those flowery, multicolored scarves.

"Yes," I told her when she asked. "Sure. Of course. I'd be happy to talk to you about my . . . *experience*."

Estelle came to my home a few days later. Her scarves were gone now. I was pleased that she no longer felt the need to hide it from me.

It was purplish brown, the size of a grapefruit attached to her neck. Disfiguring. Grotesque. Monstrous.

Her . . . *growth*.

We sat in my living room sipping cold lemonade. Discussing. Chatting. Smiling. Frowning. Dry-mouthed even with the lemonade.

Discussing my . . . *experience*.

I told her: Laryngectomy. Tracheotomy. Muteness. Coughing the tube out high into the air. The choking, suffocating feeling of clearing phlegm from what's left of your throat every morning. Pain. Weight loss. Inability to eat. Then milk shakes, applesauce, French fries—finally, thank God for French fries.

Estelle, I'm not going to bullshit you.

Estelle, it's not going to be easy. No one will understand what you are trying to say.

Estelle, get one of those magic slates kids play with.

Estelle, do you remember Brando's voice in *The Godfather*? You'll feel awful. You'll feel so vulnerable.

Pray, Estelle, pray.

Yes, her daughter says, she knows who I am. Estelle has told her all about me. I am the man, she says, who has given her mother hope.

Estelle's daughter tells me they are filling up their tank now because they're on their way to her house in Michigan. Estelle will live there with her until.

The daughter looks away. Estelle looks down.

Then Estelle whispers the word again so softly that I can barely hear its hiss: "Until."

Her daughter says, "Thank you for helping my mom." She starts the truck up. Estelle lifts her arms to hug me.

I see it again now. It is twice its previous size. No longer brownish, it is now mud black.

Estelle puts her arms around me. She is still wearing the yellow bracelet I gave her.

Estelle is smiling and trying to tell me something, but all I hear are her breaths, breaths she tries to make into words by spitting them into the air.

Her daughter translates her breaths. Her daughter says, "She's excited."

Estelle spits more words into the air.

I say, "What? I can't under—"

Her daughter says, "Big trip. She's trying to tell you she's excited about her big adventure."

The pickup pulls away. Estelle looks back, smiling her jack-o'-lantern smile, waving at me, off now—on her big adventure.

Six weeks later, the mail brings me a small envelope from Saginaw, Michigan. Inside it is a holy card dedicated to the memory of Estelle Kaczmarek . . . and a yellow LIVE STRONG bracelet.

I wear it with my other one, the one my wife gave me. I know they will keep me safe on any big adventure.

I AM AT HOLY ANGELS CHURCH on a Sunday morning, listening to a visiting priest who is saying the homily.

He is talking about Our Lady of Guadalupe. He says that while visiting the shrine and basilica in Mexico City last year, he heard Our Lady whisper something to him.

The priest whispers it now: "I am also the mother of darkness and fear. I have seen the darkness. I have felt the fear."

Chills run down my back.

I too have seen the darkness. I too have felt the fear.

But my mother holds me in her arms. She knows. She understands.

MY SON JOE is fourteen years old. He has seen me carry the cross at Holy Angels Church for six years now.

After church one Sunday he asks me, "Can I carry the cross sometime?"

I say, "Why do you want to carry the cross, Joe?"

"Because you do," Joe says.

I realize that maybe that's not the perfect answer, but it's a good start.

"Sure," I tell him.

"Great!" Joe says. He grins a big, toothy grin and I grin with him and hug him.

I have taught my son to throw a curveball. I have taught my son to shoot a jumpshot. I have taught my son to counter a left hook with a right jab. And I have taught my son to ease Christ's burden, to carry His cross.